THINKING AT THE SPEED OF BIAS

THINKING AT THE SPEED OF BIAS

How to Shift Our Unconscious Filters

SARA TAYLOR

BK

Berrett–Koehler Publishers, Inc.

Berrett-Koehler Publishers, Inc.
1333 Broadway, Suite 1000
Oakland, CA 94612-1921
Tel: (510) 817-2277
Fax: (510) 817-2278
www.bkconnection.com

ORDERING INFORMATION

Quantity sales. Special discounts are available on quantity purchases by corporations, associations, and others. For details, contact the "Special Sales Department" at the Berrett-Koehler address above.
Individual sales. Berrett-Koehler publications are available through most bookstores. They can also be ordered directly from Berrett-Koehler: Tel: (800) 929-2929; Fax: (802) 864-7626; www.bkconnection.com.
Orders for college textbook/course adoption use. Please contact Berrett-Koehler:
Tel: (800) 929-2929; Fax: (802) 864-7626.

Distributed to the U.S. trade and internationally by Penguin Random House Publisher Services.

Berrett-Koehler and the BK logo are registered trademarks of Berrett-Koehler Publishers, Inc.

Printed in Canada

Berrett-Koehler books are printed on long-lasting acid-free paper. When it is available, we choose paper that has been manufactured by environmentally responsible processes. These may include using trees grown in sustainable forests, incorporating recycled paper, minimizing chlorine in bleaching, or recycling the energy produced at the paper mill.

Library of Congress Cataloging-in-Publication Data

Names: Taylor, Sara, (Business consultant), author.
Title: Thinking at the speed of bias : how to shift our unconscious filters / Sara Taylor.
Description: First edition. | Oakland, CA : Berrett-Koehler Publishers, Inc., [2024] |
    Includes bibliographical references and index.
Identifiers: LCCN 2023058311 (print) | LCCN 2023058312 (ebook) | ISBN 9781523006762
    (paperback) | ISBN 9781523006779 (pdf) | ISBN 9781523006786 (epub)
Subjects: LCSH: Prejudices. | Discrimination. | Multiculturalism. | Organizational change.
Classification: LCC BF575.P9 T395 2024 (print) | LCC BF575.P9 (ebook) |
    DDC 303.3/85—dc23/eng/20240205
LC record available at https://lccn.loc.gov/2023058311
LC ebook record available at https://lccn.loc.gov/2023058312

First Edition

32 31 30 29 28 27 26 25 24   10 9 8 7 6 5 4 3 2 1

Book production: Westchester Publishing Services
Cover design: Ashley Ingram
Author photo: Amber Procaccini

To Emmy,

*You've added new light to my life. May this work
contribute to greater light and a better world for you.*

CONTENTS

PREFACE

Working as a diversity, equity, and inclusion (DEI) practitioner for over three decades, I became frustrated early on with the lack of practical tools I could offer to individuals and organizations that were sincerely committed to making change.

For decades, research has clearly described the negative impact of unconscious bias on everything from our individual interactions to our organizational decisions and environments and our broader systems. Evidence of inequity across those systems is also clear.

What hasn't been equally as clear is what each of us as individuals can do to counter unconscious bias and contribute to equity.

Until now.

What I offer in the pages ahead are practical tools and strategies along with a set of competencies and skills to recognize and stop unconscious bias before it can do harm.

For individuals, I connect the theory and research of unconscious bias with the developmental, ability-driven approach of cultural competence to define the skills needed to respond more effectively in an increasingly divided world. I offer practical tools and processes to recognize when our bias is in control and the strategies to shift our thinking and, eventually, our behavior.

For organizations, I connect the practice of workplace DEI with the field and approach of organizational development to offer solutions that develop and transform organizations, allowing them to become more effective and equitable.

I also draw heavily on the application of this research, theories, and practices through my work with hundreds of organizations and countless individuals through deepSEE Consulting, the DEI training and consulting firm I founded in 2002.

Both individually and organizationally, we first need to *develop* in order to make change. It's not about lack of will but developing skill.

Yes, there are those who intentionally divide, focus on othering, and intentionally work to create inequities. This book isn't for them. This book is for

- executives who are committed to transforming their organizations and willing to start with their own development;
- managers and supervisors who want to create an authentically inclusive work environment;
- DEI practitioners, committee members, and volunteers thirsty for better understanding and addressing the drivers of inequity, ready to develop and transform their organization;
- anyone in the workplace who wants to contribute to a more positive work environment, not just for others but for themselves as well;
- students and development program participants with a desire to increase their own awareness and effectiveness; and
- community leaders, activists, and volunteers with a passion for justice and equity who are willing to start with themselves and their own actions.

It's also for anyone who is frustrated with inequities and has yearned to individually contribute to greater equity; anyone needing tools to stop the automatic unconscious process that creates their thoughts and actions; anyone who wants to consistently match their positive intent with an equally positive impact; and anyone who wants to communicate and interact more effectively.

This book is about differences in the workplace. From the trivial to the significant, from those that are visible to those that are frequently unseen, from those that are marginalized to those that are centralized.

We all bring differences to our interactions, and we all, knowingly or unknowingly, experience the world through our differences, our past experiences, and our perceptions. As such, know that I write not just from my decades of experience as a DEI practitioner but also from the identity and experiences of a White, middle-aged, cisgender female. That identity has shaped my experiences and continues to do so.

You might notice that I use the pronouns *we* and *us* quite a bit. When I do, I'm not referring to only the *we* of middle-aged White women. I'm actually referring to *all* of us because these concepts of how our unconscious works and how we develop our ability apply universally, regardless of our identity. Over my decades of doing this work, I've also found that using *we* and *us* tends to make the concepts more accessible and inviting.

Some of the terms, concepts, and frameworks in the pages ahead will be familiar to readers of *Filter Shift: How Effective People SEE the World*. As my first book, *Filter Shift*™ introduced these concepts, while this book advances and deepens them. It also provides more tangible tools for individuals to develop and contribute to broader equity.

Readers of *Filter Shift* continually tell me that the stories throughout the book engaged them and allowed them to better understand the concepts. So, while *Thinking at the Speed of Bias* goes deeper into key concepts, they are illustrated through stories.

Those stories come from real situations and events. I have reconstructed them based on my memory. Aside from my husband's name, I have changed the names of all involved to provide anonymity. Some of the stories are composites of various situations and events.

Because we don't experience differences only in the workplace, those stories also go beyond the workplace. In addition to stories, perhaps more importantly, each chapter closes with tangible next steps that individuals can take to develop.

Use this book as both a guide and a workbook.

Use it to match your positive intent with an equally positive impact.

Use it to increase your awareness of your unconscious and your ability to challenge it.

Use it to break through the frustration and helplessness that a knowledge of the immensity of inequities elicits, and counter that with tangible individual action.

Use it in your organizations to create more equitable decisions, policies, and environments.

Through those tools, my hope is to empower you, the reader, to make a difference and to contribute to a more just and equitable workplace and world.

CHAPTER 1

SLOWING DOWN TO CATCH UP

Active Conscious

With cheetah-print leggings, a striped shirt, and matching gold necklace and bracelet that look more like tinsel garland than jewelry, her outfit might be considered gaudy if she weren't a preschooler. With her hair pulled back in a loose braid, she sits with three fellow classmates at a table, each with a pool of green Play-Doh and a glorious selection of Play-Doh toys, from tiny rolling pins to various stamps and carvers resembling small pizza cutters, in front of them.[1]

Across from her sits another young girl with FRIENDS emblazoned in bold purple letters across the top of her T-shirt, fittingly appearing to be more concentrated on her friend to her left and what he is stamping into his Play-Doh pool.

In his hands is what appears to be an overturned model car that he's working to envelop into the dough as he's talking to the boy across the table from him. That last classmate, intent on the cutter he's rolling across his dough as he sits in his Justice League T-shirt and khaki shorts, seems to be hyperfocusing all his attention on his creation, which still appears to be just a pool of dough.

With a full lifetime of learning and experiences ahead of them, one can imagine their potential and the many successes they can achieve, even as they are only concentrating on this immediate success of their Play-Doh creations awaiting to emerge.

What these four preschoolers don't know is that separated from them by time and space is a group of preschool teachers along with a few preschool administrators taking part in a study. Pulled from an education conference they were attending, the study participants individually watched the preschoolers in a video of 12 randomized scenarios of traditional classroom activities—both free play and structured—of 30 seconds each.

Asked to "detect challenging behavior in the classroom . . . *before* it becomes problematic," the eye movement of the teachers was then measured using eye-tracking software.[2] In addition to the varying creations in front of them, the varying hairstyles and wardrobe choices, one of the most obvious differences among the four children was their race, as two were Black and two were White.

While the scenarios presented intentionally did not contain any challenging behavior, when the teachers were asked to anticipate it, where do you think the eyes of the teachers were focused?

On the Black students.

Who were the teachers? Both Black and White.

And remember who the students were. Preschoolers playing with Play-Doh.

What Were They Oblivious To?

Were the teachers in this study intentionally discriminating? Were they bad teachers? Maybe they just didn't care about kids? Or am I trying to paint all teachers as bad?

The answer to all of the above is no. Like most of us, those teachers entered that setting with positive intent and were oblivious to their biased behavior. If you were to ask them, I bet they would say they *wanted* and *did* what was best for *all* their students, and they would sincerely feel, think, and say that . . . *consciously.*

But their conscious mind wasn't the source of their actions.

It was their unconscious Filters.

If they were unaware of their biased behavior and are typical people like the rest of us, how likely is it that any one of us would have done the same thing and, like the teachers, been oblivious to it?

Very likely.

For all of us, across professions, racial groups, generations, and genders, our Filters are what we need to pay attention to, yet they are what many of us are oblivious to.

Active Conscious

Are Filters just unconscious bias?

No.

I coined the concept of Filters and Frames using concepts from the field of psychology, cultural competence, and unconscious bias. Our Frames are the objective differences we are more conscious of. Our Filters, on the other hand, operate in our unconscious and dictate our thoughts and behaviors without our knowing. While they are ubiquitous, they remain undetected to most of us.

Residing in our unconscious, our Filters are automatic mechanisms designed to take in and process exponentially more information—both biased and neutral—than we are consciously aware of. In any given situation, within milliseconds, they select from that stored information, bias and all, screening what gets passed to our conscious mind.

In doing so, they determine our thoughts, which in turn dictate our behaviors, all without our knowing. Regardless of whether that behavior leaves a positive or a negative impact, whether it creates connection or misunderstanding, or whether it produces disparity or equity, it originated with a Filter.

Think about each step in this automated process (see figure 1.1): our unconscious Filters shape our conscious thoughts, which in turn create our externally visible behaviors or actions. In any given interaction or situation, only one of these steps can be absent. Which one is it?

It's the middle: conscious thought.

We skip that step of thought completely when we jump to an action without thinking about it, or in day-to-day rote tasks or common behaviors like greeting each other. Even if we don't skip it, many times the conscious thought is very passive, rubber-stamping what our unconscious Filters have already decided.

The irony of this missed step is that it's the most important step of all if we want to become more effective and make more equitable decisions. *Instead of being passive or even absent, as it can often be, the conscious thought needs to be strong and active.*

The **Active Conscious** is a process in which we intentionally slow down, pause, and question our Filters. Slowing down, counterintuitively, allows us to challenge this high-speed, automatic process and catch up to the speed of bias. Instead of allowing our Filters to determine our thoughts and behaviors, the Active Conscious process allows us to consciously check and challenge our Filters to determine our actions more actively (see figure 1.2).

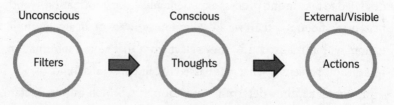

Figure 1.1   Passive Conscious Process

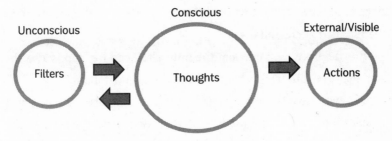

Figure 1.2 Active Conscious Process

To efficiently take in, categorize, and prioritize millions of pieces of information in milliseconds, our Filters need to be automated. Yet because that automatic process doesn't include a step to distill bias from our thoughts, we must take that step consciously in a more active process.

The Source of Our Behaviors

We are often caught by a false assumption that because our behaviors are easy to witness externally, they are what's important. Just change the behavior, then everything will be fine—tell teachers to stop looking at the Black kids when they are looking for challenging behavior, and the problem is solved! What we miss is the oak tree–like roots of our Filters in which the behavior originates, and the fact that even when we sanction a specific behavior, those Filters remain.

Let's remember, that behavior—the eye movement—that is external was created by a conscious thought, and that conscious thought was created by an unconscious Filter.

That means if I truly want to better understand others and the situations I am in, if I truly want to create equitable outcomes and even if I just selfishly want to be more effective for myself, I need to trace *both my behavior and the behavior of others* all the way back to the Filters that created them.

But the irony remains that the only often passive step is also the step that needs to be most active: the conscious thought.

We even have typical sayings that reflect this missed step. "I just wasn't thinking!" or "How could I have thought that?" Consider the infrequent high-stress scenarios where a common person suddenly steps in to be the hero, pulling a stranger from a burning car or jumping in to help someone in distress. What do they often say? "No, I didn't think about it. I just did it."

Much more frequent are the numerous actions we take every day *without* thinking. These might be

- a rote behavior I perform regularly;
- an immediate response to someone I'm in conversation with that I later regret, wishing I would have thought about it more before blurting it out;
- a behavior driven by group norms, for example, if someone I am just meeting for the first time approaches me with hand outstretched, I do the same and reach out for a handshake without needing to think about it, which makes it likely that I'll do the same thing whenever I greet someone else. And there are countless other examples.

Filters are powerful. And whether the thought is there or not, our behavior still stems from the Filter.

It's about the Filters!

When we're interacting with others, the source of what we observe externally is a Filter—their Filters.

Without the Active Conscious process, it's not only that our Filters create our behavior; they also create *perceptions* and *judgments* about what we observe externally. I might first consciously notice someone's skin color, or maybe someone else's purple spiked hair or another's significant limp. Those are their external, obvious differences, but how I perceive them, make sense of them, and judge them comes from my unconscious Filters. And if I can't step into the Active Conscious process to challenge and shift those Filter judgments about external differences, it's my Filters that continue to decide for me without my awareness.

Our Filters draw on a warehouse of our own past experiences. That's why we believe them, even if they're wrong. While our Filters are a part of us, the Active Conscious process allows us to separate from them, step to the side of them, if you will, to witness them, and, when necessary, create conscious thoughts that challenge them.

With the ability to check and challenge our Filters, we are less likely to create biased decisions or actions regardless of the differences—or similarities, for that matter—and more likely to create interactions with a positive impact that matches our positive intent.

Bring It Closer to Home

Like a joke that we already know the punch line to, it's easy to look at a study like the one at the head of this chapter and, knowing it's about bias, think, *Well, that's so obvious. I wouldn't do that.*

Because statistics say otherwise, I'd like you to imagine yourself in a specific situation, and we'll use the Active Conscious process to better understand the judgments we might make.

You're on a project team that you've been frustrated with, wanting to make a number of changes but never in the position to do so. Then you're assigned as project lead, and so you spend several hours preparing for the first meeting with your colleagues, where you will outline the changes you want to implement.

The meeting is scheduled to start at 2:00, and you work in an organizational culture where everything starts on time, so you arrive at 1:50, ready to lead your colleagues in the agenda you've prepared. Your colleagues stream into the conference room one after another, but at 2:00, your colleague Alex has still not arrived. Even though your planned agenda starts at 2:00, you wait five minutes before starting, and it's not until 2:15 that Alex finally arrives. Each of those 15 minutes you are getting more and more frustrated with their absence because they play a key role in the project.

What might be your thoughts about Alex? They

- are rude;
- don't care about the project;
- showed up 15 minutes after the start time;
- are unprofessional;
- don't respect you as the team leader;
- can't be counted on.

Left unchallenged, these thoughts would likely shape your behavior toward this colleague. In the short term, perhaps you assign them lesser responsibilities. In the long term, perhaps you don't give them an equitable role on the team, or perhaps, if the opportunity arises, you submit a negative review of them.

The Active Conscious Process

Let's walk through the specific steps of the Active Conscious process:

1. **Stop to be conscious of our thoughts**, even listing them out after the fact as we did with thoughts about Alex.

2. **Separate the thoughts that are subjective.** Those are the thoughts that Explain and Evaluate, which is the telltale sign that they are coming from our Filters.

3. **Challenge the subjective thoughts coming from our Filters** by focusing on what we are left with, the objective See or observe. Those are the thoughts that everyone, regardless of their Filters, would agree to. Almost always, those are few to none of the items on the list.

Of all the thoughts about Alex, only one is objective: *showed up 15 minutes after the start time.* The rest are subjective and shaped by our Filters, which means we don't know whether they are true. In addition, our Filters add to misunderstandings if the individual has an observable difference in identity from us, perhaps a different skin color, generation, or perceived gender.

Particularly if that different identity is unfamiliar to us, or marginalized or frequently stereotyped, we are also more likely to attribute our negative Filter judgments to that entire identity group. For example, if they are generationally a millennial, our Filters might easily leap to generalizing the judgments to the whole group: *Millennials can't be counted on, and they're so rude and unprofessional.*

The Filter Shift Process

How do we know which of these thoughts were shaped by our Filters? We can SEE our Filters by examining the thoughts they shape. To SEE (See, Explain, Evaluate) is not about ocular vision but about being able to differentiate between our objective thoughts (See) and our subjective thoughts shaped by our Filters (Explain and Evaluate).

The Active Conscious process is the key, foundational strategy we continue to use throughout a three-stage developmental process to separate biased from neutral information about our self, others, and our behaviors. We first apply the Active Conscious process to acknowledge and accept accountability for our own Filters (SEE Self). We then use the process to assume difference in other people without judgment (SEE Others), and finally, we use the process to shift our behaviors to be more effective and equitable (SEE Approach).

This three-stage process of SEE Self, SEE Others, and SEE Approach is the Filter Shift process that I detail in my book, *Filter Shift: How Effective People SEE the World* (see figure 1.3). Filter Shift is both the ability to create more effective and equitable behaviors as well as the process of development we engage in to achieve that ability and thus move from *unknowing* to *knowing* and from *ineffective* to *effective*.

This is how we slow down to catch up to the speed of bias. The ability to recognize our Filters, take accountability for them and their impact on ourselves and others, and challenge and shift them is the necessary skill we must develop to both increase our own effectiveness as well as positively contribute to a broader environment of equity.

Unfortunately, most of us have yet to develop this ability, at best creating unintentional misunderstanding and at worst, creating harm to ourselves and others.[3] That's the bad news. The good news is that any of us can consciously develop it.

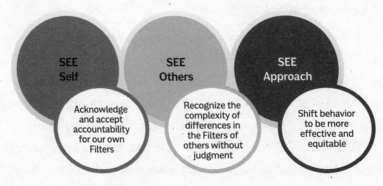

Figure 1.3   The Filter Shift Process

It's Developmental

What makes this Filter Shift process so challenging is that it's *developmental*. We'll dive deeper into the developmental process in chapter 4.

Because it's developmental, we can't skip a step or jump back and forth. An infant doesn't wake up one day with the developmental ability of a toddler and then regress to the developmental ability of an infant the next day. Likewise, they can't decide they don't want to be a "terrible two toddler," skip that stage, and go straight to kindergartner.

This sounds like common sense, yet over and over again I hear both individuals and organizations, unaware that they haven't developed through the first two stages of SEE Self and SEE Others, asking for a list of actions, which comes only in the third stage.

I call it the *Nike syndrome* because they believe they can *just do it.* They ask me: *What should I do in this situation? What should I say? How do I respond?* The answers to all those questions don't become clear until we have developed through the first two stages and have developed the ability to identify the equitable actions or effective approach.

Focusing on actions too soon, we don't realize *that* and *how* we might be ineffective.

We miss the true source, our Filters, and so we often miss the best approach. .

Organizations also fall into the trap of focusing on *doing,* on completing tasks, on taking action before they have developed, also unaware *that* and *how* those actions might be ineffective. This is why so many organizations spin their wheels in DEI with tractionless transactions.

Individuals Remain Stuck in Clueless Oblivion

We learn about this developmental process of Filter Shift through the field of cultural competence. Unfortunately, we know that most of the population hasn't developed the levels of competence that allow us to be effective as we interact across difference.[4] Again, we'll focus on that more in chapter 4.

On an individual level, most of us remain controlled by our Filters, oblivious to the reality that they're creating our thoughts and driving our behaviors. This control by our Filters is compounded by the additional reality that many of us are also oblivious to the *impact* those behaviors have on others, regardless of our identity.[5]

Even when we have positive intent, because we believe we are more effective than we actually are, we don't see the glaring need to develop.[6] That leads us to create interactions that result in misunderstanding at best, biased decisions and microaggressions at worst.

What about those individuals who intentionally divide and discriminate? With increasing polarization felt across the globe, more of us feel this increase in divisiveness, created by the control of our Filters and a lack of development.

Getting together with family? Fewer of us are choosing to do so because of political polarization.[7]

Establishing close friendships with people of a different race? Most of us don't.[8]

Experiencing hate-based incidents and violence? Twelve percent more of us are.[9]

Why? Of course, countless factors are involved, but in many cases of polarization, we can witness how an individual's unconscious Filters control their thoughts and behaviors because they lack the ability to see, challenge, and shift them.

Let's look at the example of the teachers again. Their attention was drawn to race or skin color. Yet consciously, I'm guessing they would have said, "I treat all the kids in my classroom the same, and I want what's best for all of them regardless of race."

Yet their eyes were on the Black kids.

Their Filters unknowingly misled them to believe that skin color was the important factor they needed to pay attention to. If they are like many individuals, they would have been oblivious to how their Filters attached a judgment to that specific Frame of skin color. All with the best of intentions.

The Path That Leads to Disparities

Unfortunately, it's not *only* preschoolers or teachers or *only* the education system. It's not *only* a rare phenomenon of disparities existing *only* in the United States, *only* among races.

Patterns of disparity are evidenced in all our systems and across many identities. That same evidence shows up on a more local level in organizations and groups. And, like the teachers in front of a video screen, the source of the disparities is rooted in each of us—more specifically, in our Filters. And the reality is that most of us, regardless of our identity, have not yet developed the ability to effectively shift them.[10]

Let's follow the path leading from these teachers through the entire educational system.

Like the patterns of disparate response to Black and White preschoolers in this study, other studies have found similar patterns as students age through their educational experience.

One of these was conducted by researchers at Stanford who asked teachers with an average of 14 years of experience to review two incidents of minor classroom misbehavior. Those incidents were then randomly associated with a name that is stereotypically thought of as White (Greg or Jake) or a name stereotypically thought of as Black (Darnell or Deshawn). For the exact same issues, if the name associated was perceived as Black, the teachers found them more troublesome and, after the second offense, doled out more severe discipline, including suspension, than if the name of the student was perceived as White.[11]

If those preschoolers in the first study had been in a real classroom situation, or if the names in the second study were attached to real students, what would that mean for them, for their teachers, and for the relationship between them? What patterns of advantage and disadvantage would emerge for those students? And how would those patterns snowball throughout their lives?

Just as the Black preschoolers on the video screen were more likely to be seen as a source of challenging behavior, if you are a Black student in a real-life classroom, you are more likely to be disciplined with out-of-school suspension than your White counterparts. In a one-year span, 13.7 percent of Black students, 6.7 percent of Native/ Indigenous students, 4.5 percent of Hispanic students, and only 3.4 percent of White students were suspended.[12]

If a student isn't in school, it's all the more difficult for them to graduate. While the graduation rate for White students is 90 percent, it's only 81 percent for Black students and even lower for Native and Indigenous students, at 75 percent.[13]

Let's go back to the teachers. The behavior visible in the study was the teachers' eye movement focused on the Black kids more than the White kids when observing the behaviors of those kids— judgments of behaviors created by thoughts, which were created by Filters. Those behaviors in real life would also likely lead to the Filtered behavior of suspending or expelling those same kids at a higher rate than others.

The pattern of higher suspension and expulsion rates for Black kids is the outcome that is visible on a broader level of individual schools or educational systems. When individual schools, administrators, and school systems with the best of intentions see those disparate outcomes, what do they do? They create across-the-board policies that restrict separation from the classroom for all students.[14]

If those schools and educational systems addressed the behavior and the outcome by applying an approach equal to all, why do they continue to spin their wheels, unable to gain traction to reduce educational disparities?

Because schools (a) focus on the wrong thing, missing the driver of those behaviors, which are the Filters, and (b) apply the one-size-fits-all, equality-based approach, assuming that will create equitable outcomes.

Of course, it's not just schools or school systems. It's a pattern repeated across all industries, professions, and societal systems.

The vital question we each need to ask ourselves is not *if* but *when* and *where* I am contributing to disparities in my profession, in my system, in my community?

Organizations and Systems Continue to Produce Inequities

As with education, our systems across the board churn out disparities. From health care to criminal justice to our economic systems, the inequities are clear across a wide variety of groups and identities.

At a more local level, organizations across all industries and sectors still rarely, if ever, achieve parity in representation, especially in leadership. Although White men make up only 35 percent of the population, their representation as Fortune 500 CEOs is more than two and a half times that at 90 percent.[15] The first time a Fortune 500 company appointed a Black woman CEO wasn't until 2009 (Ursula Burns at Xerox), and the first openly LGBTQ+ CEO wasn't until two years later in 2011 (Tim Cook at Apple).[16]

What got us here? The obvious reason is centuries of intentional discrimination. The less obvious is millions of hiring, promoting, and managing decisions coming from the best of intent, yet driven by Filters of stereotypes, unknowingly left unchecked. As a hiring manager in one of our programs said, "I used to say I hired the best candidate, White, Black, or Purple. But it wasn't until I developed the ability to Filter Shift that I realized I didn't even know who the best candidate was."

Environments of inclusion also remain elusive in most workplaces. Marginalized groups continue to express experiences in the workplace of being *apart from* versus *a part of*. That's true for groups from transgender to Black, Indigenous, People of Color (BIPOC), disabled, or women, and the list goes on.

Let's stop to think about it. What decides how we feel at work and how we experience a workplace? Our Filters. So, if we want to be inclusive ourselves, we will need to be able to see and respond to the Filters of others. Yet few of us are able to do so. And all too many of us also operate in an organization with an equality-based culture applying the one-size-fits-all approach, oblivious to the Filters at play.

It's not that organizations aren't trying. But for decades DEI professionals have been hard at work initiating strategies, programs, and organizational change work with little to no tangible results, stuck in tractionless transactions and unable to transform their organizations. Unless we develop the individuals in our organizations and address the bias-laden Filters at play in our organizational structures, that transformation will remain ever elusive.

Beyond Individuals to Organizations and Systems

This same Filter Shift process that applies to individuals can subsequently be applied to organizations and eventually systems as well. When those organizations and systems show evidence of identity-based inequities, at their root are the Filters of stereotypes that were left unchecked and unshifted by a passive conscious.

Organizations and systems seeking greater equity can begin by first developing the individuals within them. Once those individuals have developed the ability to Filter Shift, they then can use the Active Conscious process to identify the Filter-based practices and policies they were previously oblivious to. This insight allows them to use the Equity Framework as described in chapter 11, which applies the steps of the Filter Shift process to organizations. A guided process with expanded questions, SEE Self focuses on the organization and its culture. SEE Others is focused on the stakeholders who are frequently marginalized or forgotten, and Shift Action encompasses the new, more equitable decisions, policies, and practices.

Reflection and Action

Start paying attention to your thoughts, particularly when you notice yourself making a judgment. Over the next few days, start building the muscle of the Active Conscious. As you observe the thoughts, challenge them using the SEE (See, Explain, Evaluate) model to separate the objective from the subjective thoughts. Pay attention to any patterns you might find. Those will likely help you identify your strongest Filters.

CHAPTER 2

UNDERSTANDING HOW OUR UNCONSCIOUS CREATES BIASED THOUGHTS

To fully take accountability for our Filters and acknowledge their power to create our decisions and actions, it's helpful to understand how they work. Our Filters have evolved to function the way they do: automatically, quickly, and out of our awareness. When we understand that function and purpose, we are better able to recognize our own Filters in action, engage the Active Conscious process, and begin learning to Filter Shift.

The three functions of our Filters are:

Absorb

Analyze

Decide

Is the Talk Really Small?

"For the longest time I was resentful of him, thinking he didn't have any work to do while I was drowning in work, hardly able to keep up. Either that or he was just lazy!" Naomi, a participant in one of our trainings, was relaying the judgments she had made about her coworker. We could all sense her embarrassment overladen with a newly realized sense of guilt.

In their weekly Monday-morning project update meetings, Naomi would come with a long list of everything they needed to talk about, coordinate, and plan for the next week. She always doubted their one-hour meeting could cover it all, so she would add time limits for each topic.

Because she wanted to ensure they covered everything, she was especially frustrated when Ted would start talking about his weekend. What he and his husband had done, the continuing saga of their sick dog, and even many times about the remodeling project that was taking months longer than they thought it would. She even knew their contractors' names!

After what Naomi considered his recitation, he would ask her about her weekend. "I felt as if I had to reciprocate. Yet I didn't want to tell him about every detail of my weekend because I knew we were already 5 or 10 minutes behind on our agenda!

"I didn't have that time to waste in small talk, so I would say just a few things and then move to the agenda as quickly as I could. Sometimes before the meeting I would even plan what I was going to say about my weekend that would easily segue into the first agenda item just to get there more quickly!"

She knew they were carrying the same amount of project load, doing roughly the same amount of work, but seeing how he continually wasted time in their meetings had her believing he somehow had it easier or, as she had said, that he was just lazier.

It wasn't until she heard Ted's perspective of those Monday-morning meetings that she realized how wrong she had been. They were giving their boss a project update, and Ted shared how much he valued, even needed, that personal sharing time at the beginning of their meetings. He called it their "check-in" and told their boss, as if

Naomi felt the same, "We both have so much work to do on this project, but it's always important for us to connect with each other first."

Now relaying his perspective to the rest of the training group, we could all sense Naomi's embarrassment that she had misjudged Ted and his intent. She described what he had shared with their boss. That he used that check-in to get a sense of what was going on in Naomi's life outside of work. He described one week when Naomi had shared about her son injuring his knee at his soccer game and all the doctor's appointments she had to schedule that week.

As Ted was relaying it to their boss, he said, "I knew that was a week that I was going to have to carry more of the load because she needed to tend to her son."

Was Naomi an ogre for not realizing the personal connection Ted wanted to make during those check-ins? Was Ted insensitive because he didn't realize the stress her check-ins were causing Naomi?

No. They both came to those meetings with positive intent. They both shared the same goal of a *successful* meeting. Yet the behaviors they associated with a successful meeting were completely opposite.

Naomi got distracted by that different behavior, missing the Filters that created them.

Shared positive intent. Shared value in the outcome of a successful meeting. Different Filters, therefore different Explanations and Evaluations leading to different behaviors.

Three Key Functions

While Naomi's and Ted's Filters caused the misunderstanding, it's not because those Filters somehow malfunctioned. In fact, they were doing exactly what they were supposed to do. Specifically, our Filters have three primary functions:

1. **Absorb:** take in information without conscious awareness
2. **Analyze:** explain, evaluate, and categorize information to align with our past experiences
3. **Decide:** send information to the conscious mind in the form of thoughts, decisions, perceptions, and actions

Filters, then, are incredibly active. Through their automatic processing, they absorb, warehouse, and categorize information. Then they analyze and use that information to shape and decide our conscious thoughts, perceptions, and preferences and finally, what *others* observe, our behaviors.

Of these three functions, Naomi and Ted's situation illustrates the second one well—how our Filters explain, evaluate, and categorize. We'll get to that function, but let's start with the first.

Absorb: Take In Information without Conscious Awareness

Our brains actually take in 11 million pieces of information every second.

That immense amount of information is difficult to believe or even imagine. That's because of those 11 million pieces of information, we're conscious of only 40 at any one time.[1]

That means every second our unconscious is taking in 10,999,960 pieces of information that we aren't even aware of. Some of that information helps us to regulate our body and physically function—information such as the temperature of our environment, where our body is in time and space, and so on. But it is also information about the people around us, the billboards we pass, the images we take in, the stories on the news.

I can even consciously take in information, maybe through a movie, a newspaper article, or a social media post, and consciously redact the information, even analyze it, yet not be aware of what my unconscious Filters consumed from that source.[2]

I also can take in information that I don't consciously agree with, such as information that reinforces stereotypes and bias, even information that has a negative bias against a part of my identity.

Our Filters are the gatherers and sorters automatically collecting all that information. Yet in all that gathering and sorting, there is no distinction of whether the information is biased or not.

The question isn't *whether* biased information resides in our unconscious. It does. The question is, What are we going to do about it? Are we going to continue the unconsciously automated process, leaving our Filters in control, or are we going to challenge our Filters *consciously* and *actively*?

Analyze: Explain, Evaluate, and Categorize Information to Align with Our Past Experiences

I know it's not just Naomi and Ted. We've all been in meetings or conversations or day-to-day interactions where the other person leaves describing it as wonderful, and we describe it as a poke-me-in-the-eye experience.

As George Kelly, creator of the personal construct theory, would say, "Being in the vicinity of events does not construe experience."[3]

We all have different realities. I have a different reality from someone who grew up in the city because I grew up on a farm. I have a different reality from a man or someone who is deaf or someone who is young because I am none of those things. The list goes on and on.

That means it's our Filters that determine our experience, together with our ability to challenge them, which is based on our stage of development. And what do they use as a source? The warehouse of data they have absorbed over our lifetime, consisting only of our own past experiences, both active and passive.

Explanations, Evaluations, and Categorizations

In every moment, in any given situation, our Filters are absorbing and processing information. We can apply the SEE model (figure 2.1) using Naomi and Ted's situation to better understand what's going on.

I often refer to these as levels of observation. The first level, if you will, is **See**. It is objective information—focused on what's actually there. It's also what everyone, regardless of Filters, would agree to.

Then, our unconscious Filters take over to categorize what we are observing, first to **Explain**, to make sense of the situation based on our own past experiences, then finally to **Evaluate** by placing value or judgment on what we think we see.

See is the actual behavior. In this case, let's use Ted's behavior. What words would you use to describe it?

What I find fascinating is that even this objective first level is difficult for many to describe without the influence of their Filters. For example, many would describe Ted's behavior as small talk. "Small" in this case is an evaluative descriptor. It has connotations of trivial, unimportant, less than.

A Filter-free, objective descriptor of his behavior would be communicating personal information, typically about the events of the weekend, at the beginning of the meeting.

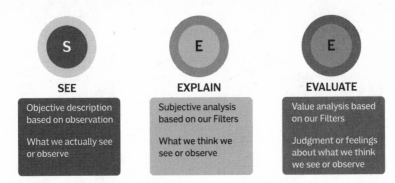

Figure 2.1   SEE Model

We know from Naomi's story that her Filters explained and evaluated that behavior as time wasting or inefficient and frustrating, while Ted described it as connecting and essential for their project work (see figures 2.2 and 2.3).

That alone is enough to create misunderstanding, but what we also heard in Naomi's confession to the rest of the training participants was something even more ineffective yet, unfortunately, very common. Her judgments didn't stop with Ted's behaviors; they extended to him holistically as a person.

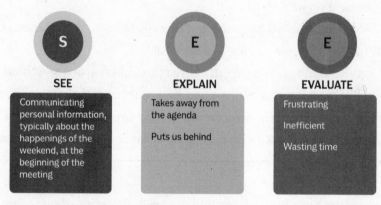

Figure 2.2   Naomi's Perspective Using the SEE Model

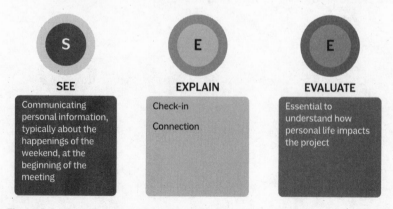

Figure 2.3   Ted's Perspective Using the SEE Model

He. Was. Lazy.

We are all in situations like Naomi and Ted on a regular basis. The second function of our Filters is to analyze the information it has already absorbed. Keeping in mind the second step of the Active Conscious process to separate subjective thoughts, we're able to consciously use the SEE model to do just that in order to more clearly understand what's *actually* going on in any situation, as opposed to what we *think* is going on.

Frames

What is it our Filters are attaching explanations and evaluations to?

Frames.

Unlike Filters, Frames are the differences we are *conscious* of. They are all the things that are objectively observable in both identity and behaviors. If a new colleague walks in the door, think of what you'll be conscious of: their size, color of skin, race, general age, gender cues.

In addition to identity-based differences, Frames are also our objective behaviors. In the case of the new colleague, it might be that they shook everyone's hand, or that they smiled.

Think about it. These are actually very few pieces of information. That's because very little of what we take in is objective. Yet we would likely leave that meeting with numerous perceptions and beliefs about the new colleague, all coming from our Filters.

In the case of Naomi and Ted, sharing personal information at the beginning of the meeting is the observable, objective Frame of behavior, and the identity-based Frame difference between Naomi and Ted was gender.

Although we don't know whether this was the case with Naomi and Ted, our Filters add to the misunderstanding when the other person's identity is different from ours, particularly when that different identity is often stereotypically marginalized. Our Filters will easily associate behaviors we don't like with stereotypes of the other identity, attaching our negative Filter judgments of the other person to that identity group as a whole.

It's about Associations

The explanations and evaluations our Filters attach to Frames aren't random. They come from well-worn pathways that have formed in our unconscious.[4]

If I said "peanut butter and...," you'd likely expect me to say "jelly" next. But if I said, "No, it's peanut butter and spinach," you'd likely pause and think I was confused. That's because our Filters have associated peanut butter with jelly numerous times throughout our lifetime of experiences and likely never associated peanut butter with spinach.

These associations form well-worn pathways in our brains. Working for decades with the Minnesota Department of Transportation as a client, I frequently use the metaphor of roads. Filter associations connect our thoughts easily and quickly to a conclusion as if they are traveling on a high-speed, multilane freeway with peanut butter on one end and jelly on the other. The connection is easy, smooth, automatic.

Without the association, the thoughts don't connect as easily. In between peanut butter and spinach is a rocky, potholed, unpaved path that makes it difficult for our thoughts to connect the two.

Let's go back to the SEE model. These associations are the unconscious explanations and evaluations our Filters have made about whatever Frames we encounter. They're based on our past experiences and all the information we've taken in throughout our lifetime. When we take in images of a particular group of people—in movies, in TV shows, on the news—and those images put that group of people in one category, we form those associations to a greater or lesser degree.

Decide: Send Information to the Conscious Mind in the Form of Thoughts, Decisions, Perceptions, and Actions

Can you tell me what your next thought will be?

If you stop to think about it, you realize you can't. None of us can.

When we become aware of this, it can be very unsettling. If *I* don't know what my next thought will be, then who does? Actually, the question is, *What* does? And the answer is: our Filters.

We know this from the field of neuroscience and the original research of Benjamin Libet of the University of California, San Francisco.[5]

Milliseconds before they pass the thought to our conscious mind, our Filters have decided for us what that thought will be, and they pass that thought to our conscious mind with full authority and be-lievability. We *think* we are in conscious control and are making our own decisions when, in actuality, we aren't.

When we put these three functions together, we see the full auto-matic process. Our Filters *absorb*, taking in exponentially more infor-mation than we are consciously aware of. They then *analyze* that information, attaching explanations and evaluations. Finally, they use those explanations and evaluations to *decide* our conscious thoughts.

We think we're in control when, if we haven't developed, it's our unconscious Filters that are in control and deciding for us.

Calling to mind the Active Conscious process (see figure 2.4), we must continue to challenge the automatic, inherently subjective process of our Filters before they create ineffective or inequitable actions.

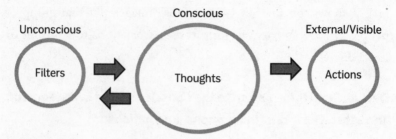

Figure 2.4   Active Conscious Process

Reflection and Action

Think of a situation where things didn't go well. It doesn't need to be recent. In fact, many times we hold on to memories of difficult situations for long periods of time. So, if the situation is from years ago, that's okay.

Take yourself through these steps:

1. **Describe the situation.** Write down your thoughts and reactions as well as the behavior of the other individual(s) involved.
2. **Circle the subjective thoughts.** Those are the thoughts that Explain and Evaluate, which is the telltale sign that they are coming from our Filters.
3. **Focus on the objective thoughts.** Those are the thoughts that are left uncircled. Remember that almost always those are few to none of the items on the list.
4. **Assume positive intent.** If it was a situation that didn't go well, chances are that your Filters negatively evaluated the other individual(s) involved. Try to assume instead that they had positive intent. Unless it was an act of intentional othering on their part, they likely did.

5. **Challenge your Filters.** If the other individual(s) had positive intent and your Filter judgments of them were negative, then the only explanation is that your Filters misled you.

6. **Use the Active Conscious process.** You know the behaviors or actions of the other individual(s), and if they had positive intent, their thoughts and Filters told them those behaviors were good, respectful, and positive. So, what might their Filters have been, and how are they different from yours?

CHAPTER 3

UNDERSTANDING THE TYPES AND IMPACTS OF FILTERS

While knowing the function of our Filters allows us to better understand how to challenge them, knowing the distinctive *types* of Filters gives us a road map to guide our development. To recognize our own Filters, we start with the types of Filters that are easiest to identify and progress to those that are the most difficult:

1. Individual Filters
2. Group Filters
3. Systemic Filters

Knowing the three types of Filters is also critical to understanding the connection between our Filters and the inequities they create in our organizations and larger, societal systems.

Selfish or Selfless?

It wasn't just a piece of candy. It was a source of learning for him later as an adult.

Like many mixed-race or mixed-culture kids, Tamim Ansary wasn't just seeing and feeling the many tangible differences between his parents' families; he was living them, being them.[1] Yet he didn't fully understand them when he was young.

I had an opportunity to hear Ansary speak many years ago. An Afghan American and writer, he spoke about his identity and said it wasn't until he was an adult that he was able to make sense of it and how he was different.

The son of an Afghan father and a mother from the United States, he grew up in Afghanistan in the family compound surrounded by cousins, aunts and uncles, and grandparents, a rich mix of generations that was all his family.

One of the things he remembered was being so confused as people from the United States continually praised him and other Afghan kids for being selfless. They would then compare them with kids in the United States whom they deemed very selfish.

"I couldn't understand because I thought of myself as incredibly selfish. It just didn't make sense."

This would particularly happen as family and colleagues of his mother would arrive from the United States with their bags of candy to distribute to the kids. Because they were unable to communicate across language barriers, they'd use the candy as a means of connecting, handing it out one piece at a time to each of the kids.

As Ansary was handed a piece of candy, he would immediately break it to give one half to his sister before eating the other half. That's when they would call him selfless and compare him with the selfish kids from the United States.

He said it wasn't until he was an adult that he fully understood. "It wasn't about being selfish or selfless. It's that *my* definition of self was different. As soon as I got that piece of candy, I made sure that *my self* had a piece."[2]

It was his Filters defining "self" as his family. Having grown up half a world away from Ansary, it's my Filters that define self as just me, an individual. Our different Filters can create very different worldviews for each of us.

Types of Filters

From Ted and Naomi in project meetings to Ansary splitting his piece of candy to the teachers watching the preschoolers, each respectively represents one of the three types or forms of Filters:

1. Individual Filters
2. Group Filters
3. Systemic Filters

In the case of Ted and Naomi, they were lucky because the Filters that were involved are some of the easiest Filters to identify and shift, *Individual Filters*. The Filters at play for Ansary were *Group Filters* and for the teachers, *Systemic Filters*.

The order of these types of Filters is important because they are progressive, not in the sense that they build on one another but that they are progressively more difficult to identify and thus shift. That's why when we work to intentionally develop our ability to Filter Shift, we start with the easiest—Individual—and eventually progress to the most difficult—Systemic.

They are also progressive in their potential to cause more harm. Naomi's Filter judging Ted's check-in time at the beginning of their meetings likely won't contribute to broader social inequities. The Systemic Filters of the teachers likely could.

If I can't acknowledge my Individual Filters, I will have an even more difficult time acknowledging my Group Filters, and it will likely be impossible for me to acknowledge that I have Systemic

Filters. Most importantly, if I can't acknowledge my Systemic Filters, I won't understand how they are connected to and reinforce the inequities in my organization and the systems around me.

Individual Filters

Some Individual Filters are as trivial as purple polka dots.

Take one look at my desk, and it will be easy to see that I prefer the color purple and polka dots. My pens, my notebook, and my phone case are all purple. Then there are the polka dot coasters and screen saver. My closet is pretty much the same, with polka dot blouses, dresses, skirts, and rompers—and of course, my favorite dress is my purple polka dot dress.

I like to be happy, and both the color purple and polka dots give me a warm feeling of joy that easily brings a smile to my face. Both consciously and unconsciously I associate purple and polka dots with joy. I'll admit that the preference is pretty trivial, but I also need to admit that this conscious preference is strongly reinforced unconsciously by my Filters, which means I might not always be aware of it.

Show up to a job interview with me, and if you're wearing polka dots or purple and if I'm not checking my Filters, the positive association I have for each of those will likely transfer to you, whether you deserve it or not.

I start with the trivial Individual Filters because they are just that. Trivial. We can all agree that wearing purple to a job interview won't inherently make you better at the job I'm hiring you for.

Making that association would be ludicrous, right?

Yet, let's go just a step further into these Individual Filters to those that aren't as trivial. Imagine Naomi was meeting Ted for the first time as she was interviewing him for a job. He continued the small talk at the beginning of their interview as Naomi was anxious to get to her questions. Would she hire him even though her Filters were telling her Ted was wasting her time and even though they associated him with laziness?

There's a chance that she wouldn't.

Just the fact that there is a chance that she wouldn't should give us pause, because the real question is, Does that small talk, like the purple polka dots, have anything to do with whether or not Ted can do the job?

Extremely unlikely.

But if we don't have the ability to challenge our Filters, something as trivial as purple polka dots or small talk could impact who gets the job.

Who does get the job? Over the years, in the numerous organizations that we've worked with at deepSEE, we've encountered many Individual Filters that have been institutionalized. Clients, with chagrin, admit their organizations' preferences and how they consciously use those preferences to justify and validate their hiring decisions. Some are common, some more obscure:

- **Graduated from a particular university:** This preference is the most common across industries and regions. After identifying this hiring preference, participants in one organization even joked about how it was present in the workplace after hiring as well, as the company would offer employees tickets to sporting events only at this specific university or celebrate the homecoming week of that university with internal workplace events.
- **Grew up on a farm:** The Filter associated at one organization was that growing up on a farm meant they were hard workers and therefore better candidates.
- **Was in the Peace Corps:** An international development organization justified this preference, saying it meant the

candidate had experience living in a different culture. Yet they didn't give the same preference for others who had a similar experience outside the Peace Corps.

More Than Just Polka Dots

These Filters aren't all trivial like my preference for polka dots. They can also feel as if they are a foundational part of our identity. Personality types are an example.

If I weren't an extrovert, I don't know if I would recognize myself. It is who I am.

Whether that personality comes to me from nature versus nurture is not the debate important to us as we understand our Filters. What *is* important is that this individual Filter determines how I perceive others and how I show up in the world.

And, as much as it is a part of me, it's also a Filter I can shift to be more effective.

- I can challenge it in the job interview and make sure it doesn't influence my judgments about candidates—either positively for extroverts or negatively for introverts.
- I can recognize it as I plan for team meetings and make sure I'm considering a meeting that fits an introversion preference as much as my extroversion preference.
- I can acknowledge its role or potential influence in the longer-term relationships I develop with my staff and make sure that doesn't cloud my judgment when I make a decision about promotions.

There are so many models or theories that help us identify our preferences, from our Myers-Briggs personality type to our Clifton-Strengths (StrengthsFinder strengths), from our Kolbe A Index or

DiSC to our Love Languages and more. Because our Individual Filters are essentially our preferences, these models help us identify our Individual Filters and consciously acknowledge our own differences as just that—differences.

That acknowledgment, in turn, allows us to detach a bit of our judgment from the behaviors driven by our Individual Filters so we can be more objective and not see those behaviors as good or bad, but just different.

Why Are Individual Filters Easy to Identify?

Again, to better understand and challenge our Filters, it's easiest to start with the Individual Filters. These are the easiest to identify for three reasons. First, we likely consciously agree with the Filter. Ask Ted if small talk is good, and he'd say yes. He may even say that he intentionally creates it.

The other reason these are easy to identify is because we can more easily see that the association the Filter is making might not be true; it might even be ludicrous. That makes it easy for us to challenge the Filter.

While individual, these Filters are not unique. There are patterns of similar preferences found in millions of people. Yet I call them Individual because these Filters don't significantly correlate to identity groups or Frames. You don't find that 90 percent of extroverts are women while 90 percent of introverts are men, as an example.

That's another reason why they are easy to identify, because when they aren't typically tied to one specific Frame or another, we don't hesitate as much in identifying them or calling them out.

Let me say that another way. When people in *my own* group, people I share a Frame with (gender, race, nationality, generation, etc.), exhibit the difference of an Individual Filter, it can be easier to acknowledge the different behavior without judgment and therefore easier to shift our own behavior.

Less Significant

Individual Filters are also less significant when it comes to systemic inequities because there typically isn't a correlation between the two. We don't see, for instance, that of those who hold the most wealth or positions of power and advantage, 90 percent love purple, or any other color, for that matter. They aren't all small-talkers or all introverts, as an example.

Easier to Address

Because we can be more conscious of Individual Filters and because they don't tie to group identities, they are typically easier for people to discuss, easier to refrain from judgment, and easier to shift. As an example, I frequently hear participants talk about how they adjust their meetings to accommodate both introverts and extroverts.

Because they are easier to identify, talk about, and shift, they are a great starting point in our developmental process.

Group Filters

Unlike Individual Filters, our Group Filters are shaped in, for, and by the groups we are part of to create shared meaning. Oftentimes they are shaped over long periods of time as a means of establishing social norms or expectations for our behaviors.

An easy-to-see example is how we greet each other. In some parts of the world, it's a kiss on the cheek. In other parts it's a handshake, and in others it's a bow. Different behaviors, but in all cases, we don't stop to think about how to greet someone; our Filters just decide for us.

To understand Group Filters, we look to the field of cultural competence, starting with the definition of culture. Janet and Milton Bennett define culture as shared meaning, experiences, and perspectives.[3] Remember what gathers our experiences and creates our perspectives? Our Filters. Culturally, we then share with our groups the meaning our Filters attach to those experiences and perspectives. The meaning, experiences, and perspectives then reside in our Filters. And what do our Filters create? Our thoughts and behaviors.

So, when a group shares Filters, they share the same expectations for behaviors. Just think about small groups you're part of and the expectations and behaviors you share:

- The book club that rarely if ever discusses the book because they always start with wine and time to catch up
- The family that always sits down together for dinner, regardless of different schedules
- The work team that makes a point to celebrate a win every week
- The friend group that always teases each other with sarcasm

We typically teach about these Group Filters by looking at bigger groups—one country versus another or one generation versus another, as an example. We also identify them by what is visible or external: the behaviors that are more prevalent in that group. For instance, one book club rarely talks about the book, while another book club only talks about the book.

Here are some examples of Group Filters easily observed in different country cultures or different generations. But before reading them, it's important to remember that these are patterns of tendency, *not* absolutes. That is, not everyone from the same country or generation shares the same cultural Filter to the same degree. But the pattern is more prevalent in their group than others.

Examples of Group Filters:

- People from the World War II generation *tend to* be more formal than Generation Zers.[4]
- Boomers *tend to* care more about their title and hierarchy, while Gen Xers *tend to* not place much value in either.[5]
- As illustrated in Ansary's example, people from Afghanistan, along with most other countries in the world, *tend to* be much more group oriented than people from the United States, Scandinavia, or the United Kingdom, who are more oriented to the individual.[6]
- Folks from Finland *tend to* be more equality oriented, while people in India *tend to* be more status oriented.[7]
- In Japan, people *tend to* be more focused on relationships, while in Germany, people *tend to* be more focused on tasks.[8]
- Spaniards *tend to* be more emotionally expressive, while Japanese *tend to* be more emotionally restrained.[9]

And the list goes on and on. The book *Kiss, Bow, or Shake Hands* is a great resource if you want to dive into these Group Filters more.[10]

Why Are Group Filters More Difficult to Identify?

Group Filters are more difficult to acknowledge than Individual Filters for a couple of reasons. First, unlike Ted and Naomi, who might see a variety of differences in their coworkers when it comes to small talk, those differences aren't tied to identities—that is, 90 percent of those who prefer small talk aren't from the same generation or the same race or gender. Group Filters, on the other hand, *are* shared by an identity or cultural group.

Because we share the same meaning, experiences, and perspectives with our group, the behaviors created by that shared meaning become expected—they're "just the way we do things around here."[11]

I see those behaviors around me all the time in the groups I am part of, so they are the norms or the default modes I have come to expect.

I often think about it with the analogy of fish. Our culture is the water we swim in, yet we don't even know that we're in water, much less that there is such a thing as air or land. Swimming is the only behavior we know because it's the behavior that fits our culture.

The second reason Group Filters are more difficult to identify is because that lack of exposure to different behaviors can lead me to be even more judgmental when I see them, dismissing them as just wrong. If you talk to me, a fish, about that walking and flying stuff, what am I likely to say?

Nope. Those are just wrong.

We mistakenly believe our cultural behaviors are the good, right, and respectful behaviors. Different cultural behaviors, then, aren't different. They're just bad, wrong, and disrespectful.

And what convinces us of that misperception? Our Filters.

Conscious yet Judgmental

As with Individual Filters, we can more easily be conscious of the behaviors our Group Filters create. Ask people whether they are direct or indirect communicators, as an example, and they will likely be able to tell you. However, because Group Filters are tied to group norms, removing judgment from those behaviors is more difficult.

In training sessions when we talk about communication styles, we repeat that one isn't *better* or the *right* behavior. Nonetheless, there will still be the occasional participant who will make a statement akin to,

"But we can't have that kind of varied communication in the workplace. That would just be unproductive and disrespectful."

More Powerful Than Purple Polka Dots

Group Filters also have more power to create harm than Individual Filters.

While Individual Filters can dictate my behavior and may even lead me to unknowingly offend someone, their power ends there, with me as an individual. We don't have a recent history of treating people who love purple differently. We don't see patterns of advantage or disadvantage for purple lovers, or those who love small talk, for that matter, in our societal systems. Their power ends with my individual actions. It doesn't connect to broader systems.

That's not the case with Group Filters or Systemic Filters.

That's because both Group Filters and Systemic Filters can reinforce stereotypes, just in different ways and to varying degrees.

Broader Judgment of Stereotypes

Let's start with what stereotypes are. They are broad-brushstroke judgments about a specific identity. They have three key ingredients: they are good or bad evaluations, they are very simplistic evaluations, and they are attached to a whole identity group and everyone in it. There is no variation, no deviation. Because the brushstrokes are broad, they obscure any complexities of a full group of people.

All of X Group Are Lazy. All of Y Group Are Smart.

How can our Group Filters reinforce stereotypes? Essentially, our Filters can see the behavior of another person and attach a judgment to that behavior but then transfer that same judgment to the identity of that person. We conflate the behavior and identity under the same judgment, particularly if the judgment of the behavior matches a stereotype already forming one of our unconscious Filters.

Moving Away from Broad-Brushstroke Judgment

Our challenge, then, is how to identify and talk about our differences, well, *differently*.

Take a look again at all my examples of Group Filters. We allow for variation and deviation when we recognize tendency. In addition, all the descriptors are nonjudgmental. Formal or informal: neither is good or bad.

If you perceive one or the other as better, that evaluation is actually coming from your Filters. And remember, when that judgment is attached to a particular identity or Frame that is often stereotypically marginalized, we are also more likely to attach our negative Filter judgments of that Group Filter not only to that person but also to that identity group as a whole, unconsciously reinforcing stereotypes we may well swear consciously that we don't support.

If there were two people in a room, one from the WWII generation and the other a millennial, would you be able to tell the difference as soon as you walked in the door? Of course you would. That's because the two have very different Frames—identity differences that we are conscious of and that are often easy to observe.

And each of those Frames have stereotypes attached to them.

Our Filters jump to associating that judgment more broadly with everyone who shares that Frame. They jump to *all* millennials, in this case, that *all* millennials are rude, not that their behavior is informal, or that *all* World War II veterans are stuffy, not that their behavior is formal.

How quickly our Filters jump to associate judgment.

How quickly our Filters reinforce stereotypes.

If I'm not able to acknowledge and challenge my Filters, I may be the one unjustly labeling another as rude or stuffy. I may be the one who is unintentionally offending or even causing harm.

What's important for us to remember when we are interacting with someone with a distinctly different Group Filter is that the be-havior that our Filters tell us is right, good, or professional is actually just *different*.

Systemic Filters

Systemic Filters have more power than either of the other two types of Filters.

While Group Filters may at times reinforce stereotypes as a *second-ary* step, Systemic Filters are a *primary source* that *always* reinforces stereotypes. For Group Filters, the judgment starts with the behavior of others and has the potential to transfer that judgment to identities. But Systemic Filters start by placing that judgment on the identity itself.

Systemic Filters also have been supported by systems throughout history to both intentionally and unintentionally create advantage for some of those identities and disadvantage for others. Because they are held by a significant number—often the majority—of indi-viduals, their power extends into the groups and systems in which we all find ourselves operating.

With Systemic Filters, we typically have no conscious awareness of them. In fact, we may consciously disagree with them! That's what makes them more difficult to address. Just as we learn from cultural competence to understand Group Filters, we learn from the field of unconscious bias to understand our Systemic Filters.

Associations

Systemic Filters are essentially stereotypes created by unconscious associations.

As we know, the source of all our visible, external behavior is our unconscious Filters. When those Filters are stereotypical, the behavior they create aligns with those stereotypes, good or bad.

Unlike Group Filters, Systemic Filters don't judge the behavior first; they just judge the identity. Not only do stereotypes not allow for deviation, they also don't allow for complexity. For example, everyone in X group is lazy, and there is no other descriptor for the whole group or identity, no other Explanation or Evaluation.

That's because the associations are so strong. The freeway that the associations travel on has been established through years of experiences taking in movies, TV shows, news clips, and advertisements.

Remember peanut butter and ... jelly? There's actually a test that measures these unconscious associations, but not for peanut butter—for people. It's the Harvard Implicit Association Test (IAT). It tests our unconscious associations with different identities such as race, gender, sexual orientation, and religion. Essentially, it measures them by how quickly we connect two concepts, like peanut butter and jelly. The faster we connect them, the stronger the association.

When the IAT tests associations with people, it tests them in comparison to stereotypes or a general evaluation for that group.

Harvard, in their research-based perspective, has done a great job of gathering data from the millions of folks who have taken their IAT and has shared those results. Those results reveal that the vast majority of people have stereotypical biases.[12]

Here are some examples:

- Seventy-eight percent of people prefer abled people over disabled people (*n* of nearly 306,000).[13]
- Seventy-three percent associate Black Americans with weapons and White Americans with harmless objects (*n* of 530,817).[14]

- Seventy-five percent associate men with career and women with family (n of 846,020).[15]
- Sixty-four percent prefer straight people over gay people (n of 1,425,486).[16]

Filters Hide from Us

She was adamant. There was no possibility that she could have this bias. As a woman who started her engineering career in the 1970s, when she was the only female engineer in her department and women were still expected to be the secretaries there, Christine wouldn't believe the results of her IAT.

"I've spent my whole career advocating for and recruiting women in engineering. Then, I take the IAT that tells me I associate men, not women, with science. It just can't be right!"

I reminded her that the IAT measures what is in her unconscious mind, not her conscious mind, and that the two may not necessarily agree. I also reminded her of the first function of Filters—that is, to take in exponentially more information than we are conscious of.

Then I asked her if she sees more men than women portrayed as scientists in movies and TV shows. In her office every minute of every day, did she see significantly more male than female engineers?

The answer to both, of course, was yes. On a moment-by-moment basis, her unconscious was getting filled to the brim with information that associated men with science. It didn't matter that her conscious belief was different.

That's another aspect of Systemic Filters that makes them both more powerful and more difficult to acknowledge. Not only do we consciously not see them, but we also consciously deny their existence. In a sense, that gives them full rein.

Given that first function of our Filters, like this woman engineer, any of us can unknowingly be taking in information that aligns with a stereotype about our own identity. Look back at the list of IAT results. It's very likely that in that high percentage of individuals who hold the stereotypes, you'll find individuals *from the stereotyped group*.

Like that woman engineer, I too have had a career all my adult life. I too have advocated for women in the workplace, and I too showed up with an unconscious association of women with family and men with career when I last took that particular IAT.

So, if almost all of us have stereotypical associations, as evidenced by the IAT, that means almost all of us have Systemic Filters. Because most folks can't challenge and shift those Filters, those stereotypes are able to seep into our behaviors, our organizational decisions, and our systems without our knowing.

According to Harvard, "Studies that summarize data across many people find that the IAT predicts discrimination in hiring, education, healthcare, and law enforcement."[17]

Notice one other commonality in this list? The Systemic Filters reinforce advantage for dominant groups, associating them with being good, intelligence, leadership, and so on. When they reinforce advantage for dominant groups, they also reinforce disadvantage and otherness for nondominant groups, thus contributing to and reinforcing systemic inequities.

What is a surprise to many is that because our Filters are absorbing more information than we are conscious of, even if we are in a nondominant group, we can hold stereotypes about our groups in our unconscious, even though we don't consciously agree with them.

It's important to point out that none of us is exclusively in a dominant group or nondominant group, for that matter. As we move through different settings and contexts, the differences in those situations shift and thus our position of dominant or nondominant can also shift. In one setting, for example, I may be the only woman on a team of all men. In another setting, I may be one of many White people in a group with few people of color.

Be it differences in religion, race, education, gender, age, physical ability, or otherwise, we all have an opportunity to be in a dominant group at one time or another. Some of us just happen to have more of that opportunity than others depending on our identity.

Reflection and Action

- Remember that our Filters create our thoughts, which in turn create our actions. So, to identify our Filters, we can look at the behaviors we tend to prefer. Imagine you were creating a guidebook for others, *How to Work with Me* or *How I Like to Communicate*. What would you put in that guidebook? It's likely that many of those behaviors and preferences would be driven by your Individual and Group Filters.
- Another way to identify our Individual or Group Filters is to think about the behaviors in others that bother you most. Maybe they're your pet peeves, or maybe you find them rude or uncomfortable. As an example, if you find indirect communication disrespectful, then your communication Filter is likely direct communication.
- Over the next several days, pay attention to both your preferences and your pet peeves to continue building your awareness of your Filters.

UNDERSTANDING YOUR STAGE OF DEVELOPMENT

The vast majority of us lack the ability to acknowledge and shift our Filters in order to be more effective and create equity. That's the bad news.

The good news is any of us can develop that ability, and we look to cultural competence to learn how.

Hi! My Name Is Joe

They were like most of the mission groups that came to Amiama Gomez. They arrived in a caravan of new Land Cruisers, parked in front of the school to hand out toothbrushes or medicines, took pictures with the kids, and left after a few hours.

By this time, after living in the community in the southwestern region of the Dominican Republic (DR) for almost two years, I had seen the same predictable pattern play out a few times already.

This particular group from central Indiana had contacted me through the Peace Corps before their arrival, asking if they could meet with the farmers' group I had been working with. After their predictable stop at the school, they wanted to meet with the group to give them a donation for their irrigation project.

The farmers' group had been preparing for days in anticipation, making sure all the members would be there in their Sunday best, divvying up roles for who would say and do what.

The open-air community center had been swept and scrubbed, and the members arrived early to gather tables and chairs from all the nearby neighbors. Doña Altagracia, who lived next door, supplied her customary thermos of coffee with dozens of espresso cups ready for the missionary guests.

As the missionaries filed out of their Land Cruisers and into the community center, I greeted them and stood at the ready to translate. All to be left baffled at what ended up transpiring.

The DR is a Spanish-speaking country. No one in Amiama Gomez spoke English except me. So, you can imagine my surprise, moments after the missionaries' arrival, when I saw one of the older men from Indiana speaking with a cluster of the farmers. My first thought was that I was impressed that this man spoke Spanish because that was rare in the missionary groups coming to the community.

Yet as I approached, what I heard was all in English.

"Hi! My name is Joe," said the man, exuding excitement as he reached out to shake the hand of Cesar, one of the leaders of the group. "Thanks so much for having us! This is so nice of you to have coffee ready for us and to show us your village."

Then, hand outstretched, turning to Bienvenido, the youngest member of the group, "Hi!" with the same exuberance . . . the same English. "My name is Joe! I hear you're all farmers! Salt of the Earth, farmers! My grandpa was a farmer. Such hard workers. Thanks for having us!"

Beaming smile, assertive approach, Joe wasn't looking to me or one of his fellow missionaries to translate.

By this time, he had been in the country for several days, seeing all the billboards in Spanish, hearing the music in Spanish blaring in the streets, hearing people at their hotel or on the streets conversing in Spanish. Yet he was oblivious. Oblivious to an easy-to-see, easy-to-hear difference of a completely different language. Oblivious to an obvious Frame.

Whoosh! Over his head—the difference didn't even enter his conscious mind.

You can imagine the response from Cesar and Bienvenido, as this hand-shaking, babbling-in-English, beaming-about-who-knows-what missionary approached them. They followed a lead they didn't understand, moving their hands up and down with his, bewildered smiles on their faces.

When asked later about the farmers and the community, Joe's eyes raised side to side as if he was searching for the answer to emerge from the clouds. "It was . . ." He continues to search. "They were . . ." Still searching. "It was . . . nice. Nice! It was nice."

A Both/And

Why was Joe so oblivious? Why did Joe have to search for a response? Why couldn't he say more than "nice"?

Because of his stage of development.

Cultural competence has identified six stages of development in how we take in and respond to differences, from oblivious, like Joe, to highly effective. Like first- through sixth-grade math, the ability of each stage can be described and measured. Also, like math, if you want to progress, specific homework can be prescribed to help you develop.

Developing and understanding our Filters are a both/and. They are two sides of the same coin. That is, in order to see our Filters, we need to develop, and in order to develop, we need to see our Filters.

Think about it like the amateur carpenter looking for a course to improve their carpentry skills. They need to understand the various tools they use, and they also need to know their current level of carpentry skill so they take the course appropriate for their level.

Remember the George Kelly quote? "Being in the vicinity of events does not construe experience."[1]

It is a combination of our Filters and our stage of development that determines our experience by linking them to our past experiences.

Let's go back to Joe and the mission group. Pretend that when we asked Joe about his experience, we also asked four others in his mission group about their experiences. What might they say?

I'm going to list real quotes that I have heard people, particularly from the United States, say about their experiences of the DR. Having lived there, having a husband from there, and having decades of back-and-forth travel to the country, I've heard lots of people express their thoughts about their experiences with the DR. But let's hypothetically say the people I'm quoting were in the same mission group as Joe, and I'm going to list them with his response. I'm listing them in a particular order, so pay attention to the pattern.

- "It was nice. Nice! It was nice."
- "Ick! It was so dirty! There were goats and pigs walking across the road. There was garbage everywhere. It was just ew!"
- "Ya know, wherever you go, you might see people that are different, but this trip just affirmed that those differences don't matter. White, Black or whatever, we're all the same human race."
- "I just kept seeing so many ways I was different, and my preferred response wasn't the typical."
- "It was so great, but I was also mentally exhausted. Every day I was taking in so much that was different. I love all of those differences, but I just didn't know what to do or how to respond."

- "My experiences? I don't have much time to tell you everything, so I'll just mention one thing and that is that it was great to step into spaces that were so expressive. I got used to expressing myself with bigger body language and a bit louder voice."

Six people in the same *event* of the mission trip with six very different experiences. Was it the DR that shaped their experience?

No. It was their stage of development.

In fact, these responses are in developmental order from Joe's oblivious response, reflective of the first stage, to the last, more complex response, reflective of the sixth stage.

Let's relate that to our day-to-day experiences. Unless we're interacting with a mirror all day, we are interacting across differences. When things don't go well in those interactions, whom or what do we typically blame? The other person or the difference itself. In reality, however, our experience with those differences, our effectiveness as we interact with them, is determined by *our own ability* to Filter Shift, regardless of what the difference is—that is, to move to an Active Conscious process in order to recognize the Explanations and Evaluations of our Filters, followed by our ability to challenge those subjective judgments and to shift our behavior to be most effective as we respond and interact across those differences.

Think Math

When we look at our broader development, we can recognize the progression from a focus on Frames that we are conscious of to a focus on Filters that operate in our unconscious. Joe hadn't even taken in the easy-to-see and easy-to-hear differences of Frames, so when asked, he didn't have a reference point to connect to. That's because he had only developed to the first stage.

These stages are developmental. Think about them as any other skill you develop. As I mentioned earlier, let's use an analogy of first-through sixth-grade math.

- **We can develop:** Just because a student tests at the second-grade level today doesn't mean they are unable to learn math and progress to the sixth-grade level. *Any of us can develop our proficiency of interacting across difference.*
- **We can test:** Want to know what grade level a student or classroom is at? Give them a math test. *There's a valid, reliable assessment that measures exactly what stage we have developed to, called the Intercultural Development Inventory or IDI.*[2]
- **We can assign homework:** Once that student tests at the second-grade level, there is specific homework for them to develop proficiency. If they do that homework, they can learn and move to the next grade. *We know the developmental strategies—essentially the homework—necessary to move from one stage to another.*
- **We can't skip a stage:** The math student can't skip learning addition and subtraction before learning equations; the skills of each grade build on one another, so none of them can be skipped. *As much as we'd like to wave a magic wand and just move everyone to the last stage, we can't. There is a developmental progression that we all must move through.*
- **We don't operate in multiple stages:** The third grader who takes a math test might get a couple of second-grade problems wrong or even a couple of fourth-grade problems right. But overall, the test places them firmly in the third grade. *The same is true for this ability to Filter Shift. We can identify the stage we have developed to and are operating in.*

- **We rarely regress:** A sixth grader doesn't suddenly lose all the math skills they have developed and have to go back to learning the basic math facts of second grade. *It is very rare that we regress, and when we do, it is more because of significant life stresses, not because we have lost the ability.*
- **We have a choice:** Any student can be adamant in believing that math isn't important and choose not to learn. *Any of us can choose to stay with our status quo level of effectiveness or choose to be more effective.*

It's Developmental

If you're like the enthusiastic math student, ready to dive in and become proficient in this ability, there are three basic concepts you need to understand: (1) what the stages of development look like; (2) the developmental strategies to move from one stage to the next; and (3) how our awareness and proficiency with Frames and Filters plays a role in our development.

Let's start with the stages themselves.

In cultural competence, there are three primary models we can learn from: Milton Bennett's Developmental Model of Intercultural Sensitivity,[3] Terry Cross's Cultural Competence Continuum,[4] and the Intercultural Development Continuum by Mitchell Hammer.[5] I use these models as a foundation, but I have created my own model that reflects what I witness over and over again as individuals develop, what they are aware of, and what they need to develop to the next stage.

The stages progressively reflect our developing ability to interact effectively across differences, beginning with the less-effective stages (see figure 4.1). *Regardless of our identities or the level of power given us* in our social systems, for us to develop, we must all progress through these stages in order, and we all are currently operating at the stage

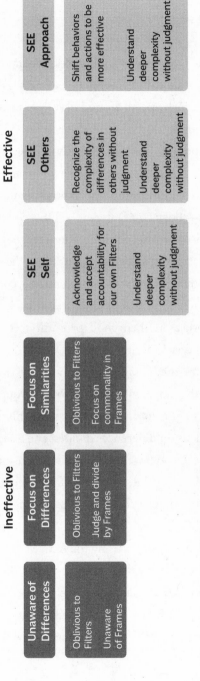

Ineffective

Unaware of Differences	Focus on Differences	Focus on Similarities
Oblivious to Filters	Oblivious to Filters	Oblivious to Filters
Unaware of Frames	Judge and divide by Frames	Focus on commonality in Frames

Effective

SEE Self	SEE Others	SEE Approach
Acknowledge and accept accountablity for our own Filters	Recognize the complexity of differences in others without judgment	Shift behaviors and actions to be more effective
Understand deeper complexity without judgment	Understand deeper complexity without judgment	Understand deeper complexity without judgment

Figure 4.1 The Filter Shift Stages of Development

we have developed to. Unfortunately, most people have developed only to the third stage.[6]

1. Stage one—Unaware of Differences: We start unaware even of Frames that are easy to take in consciously. For example, even though Spanish was all around him, Joe wasn't picking up on that difference.
   - Development: Start consciously taking in easy-to-see differences that don't even require a human interaction, such as different cultural food or entertainment.
2. Stage two—Focus on Differences: Once we start taking in the differences of Frames, our Filters do what they are supposed to do. They categorize and judge them. This is the stage of believing and reinforcing stereotypes and intentional, conscious beliefs of denigration or superiority—again, regardless of our identity. We see the world as us/them good/bad. You can hear that judgment in the missionary's response to the DR: "Ick! Ew!"
   - Development: Focus on commonality and similarities to reduce the judgment placed on other groups.
3. Stage three—Focus on Similarities: The mindset of this stage is that a focus on differences divides, and a focus on similarity unites. We believe we're more alike than different and that shared universal values guide us all and help us to resolve any misunderstanding. What we then miss is the multitude of complex differences.
   - Development: Begin using the Active Conscious process to witness our own Filters and the power they have to create our thoughts, decisions, and behaviors.
4. Stage four—SEE Self: We fully acknowledge and accept accountability for our Filters and can see how they impact every interaction.

- Development: Practice identifying the complexity of Filters of others without judgment.

5. Stage five—SEE Others: We recognize the complexity of the Filters of others without judgment. This is much more complex than recognizing the easy-to-observe differences in the Frames of others.

   - Development: This is where we move to actions. How do I shift my Filters to be more effective?

6. Stage six—SEE Approach: We are able to adjust our behaviors to match our positive intent with an equally positive impact.

   - Development: There is no developmental strategy because this is the last stage. However, we still need to work to sustain our effectiveness.

Stuck in the Third Stage

These Filter Shift stages of development are research-based stages, and remember, there's an assessment that indicates the stage to which we have developed according to the Bennett and Hammer models. What we know from millions of individuals who have taken that assessment is that most of us have only developed to the third stage, the last of the ineffective stages.[7]

Because most of us have only developed to the third stage, and because we have seen so much more evidence of the second stage in the last decade or so, I'm devoting the upcoming chapters to those stages.

My Spaghetti

I want to use an example from a story I shared in *Filter Shift* because it helps us to understand so many concepts related to development. At this time, decades ago, I had only developed to the third stage of this model. Keep that in mind with this story because the mindset of this stage is evident.

One evening, amidst the chaos of making dinner, starting the bath and bedtime routine, and simultaneously checking the kids' homework, my mother-in-law's meds, and my work emails, my husband Miguel mouthed to me from across the room with exaggerated lips, "We have to talk."

As he pulled me aside, Miguel whispered, "Mom really doesn't like your spaghetti. I don't think you should make it anymore."

My mother-in-law, Esmeralda, had been living with us for a few months. By that point the novelty had worn off, and the stress of sharing our home was starting to rise.

She had extended her visit from the DR indefinitely following a fateful afternoon when the doctors told us she had stage III breast cancer. Her treatment was aggressive with both chemotherapy and radiation. She was sick, and our house was a stressful place.

Between trying to care for her and our three young kids and balancing full-time jobs, my husband and I were having a tough time keeping up with everything. Because I had a little more flexibility in my job, it was also up to me to get her to almost daily appointments in the middle of my own work schedule.

Those are all big things to deal with. But now, it was my spaghetti too?

Now is when I should probably insert a disclaimer about my behavior because I'm not proud of my response. Yes, I was stressed, but what most influenced my self-centered reaction was my Filters. At the time I didn't understand them, so they had free rein. In fact, I'd like to think that it was my Filters and not me that responded in that moment.

I didn't acknowledge her sickness. I didn't think about how awful it would be for someone who was so ill to have to eat anything

I cooked, much less my spaghetti from a jar, particularly when she was sick.

Instead, all I could say was, "If she can't come to me and tell me to my face that she doesn't like my spaghetti, then the problem doesn't exist!" And I probably said it with jutting chin, pursed lips, and sassy neck swaying.

It's not that I was particularly attached to my spaghetti. Like everyone else in my family, I too suffered through my jar-dumping, box-opening style of cooking that I relied on at the time. I just couldn't believe that she was going to my husband to complain.

And that's how I saw it—a whiny complaint. From the view through my Filters, she didn't really want to resolve the issue. If she did, she would have come directly to me and talked to me about the problem. We would discuss it calmly and then work toward a resolution. When she instead went to my husband, well, that could only mean she was just whining and complaining. If she really wanted to resolve things, she would have come to me.

So I waited.

I waited for her to approach me directly so I could figure out what she did like to eat. As far as I was concerned, the ball was in her court because *she* was the one with the problem.

And I waited.

She didn't come to me, and I was getting more and more bothered by the situation. After all, this was our family and our home. I didn't want conflict in our midst. I was bothered enough that I wanted to talk with someone about it, someone who could help me figure out whether I was wrong in waiting for her to talk to me.

Whom did I consult?

I didn't consult another Dominican woman like Esmeralda, who might share her perspective and give me some insight. No, I talked to someone just like me. Fern, my college roommate, is another White woman who grew up in small-town Minnesota. I knew she was a *good communicator* like me.

After I relayed the situation and my response to it, I got the gratification I needed as she said, "You are so right! I say that all the time. If you can't tell me directly what's wrong, how am I supposed to know?"

Score one for me. I was right. My mother-in-law was wrong.

I honestly don't remember what happened next or if I ever made my spaghetti again, but I do remember that one minor situation didn't help our relationship. As I reflect now, I realize it wasn't the situation itself because we were in agreement: even I don't like my spaghetti.

We were in a Filter fight.

Our Filters put us there just as much as my stage of development. Operating in the third stage, I assumed we would see the same behavior in the same way. Oblivious to my Filters, I missed how they were actually driving the situation.

Esmeralda's Filters were telling her that to respect me, she needed to indirectly tell me about my spaghetti through Miguel. She was an indirect communicator. That was her Frame, the behavior I could easily see.

Unfortunately, I couldn't see that Frame without bias because I could only see it through my Filters. Those Filters were telling me that there was only one way to communicate respectfully, and that was to be direct.

Frame: direct communication. Filter attached to that Frame: respect.

When I saw the opposite Frame, indirect communication, I automatically assumed it had the opposite Filter attached to it. For me, indirect communication meant Esmeralda was disrespecting me.

In actuality, when she communicated indirectly through Miguel, she did so because she respected me too much to tell me to my face. For her, direct communication was disrespectful.

We were both responding based on our cultural Filters.

I grew up with my mother telling me to stop whining when I went to her with a complaint about my brother (and it would have only been one specific brother of all my nine siblings I would have complained about). "Talk to him yourself."

The message was clear: if the problem is between the two of you, don't involve me; deal with it yourself.

Years later, in the work world, I was told over and over again that it was company policy to handle any conflicts respectfully by going directly to the individual involved.

Esmeralda was taught exactly the opposite.

She was encouraged to use a third party as a mediator or, if you ended up in a face-to-face discussion, to use stories and metaphors to address the conflict more softly and respectfully.

Esmeralda isn't alone. In fact, much of the world teaches and prefers the indirect style of communication. Their Filters tell them that indirect communication is what is respectful.

The problem is that this association happens unconsciously. We aren't aware that our Filters make these decisions, particularly when we've only developed to one of the first three stages. A judgment is made, and the case is closed before it's sent to our conscious mind. Those decisions and judgments are based on and confirm our past experiences, which is why we trust them. Certain behaviors are good, right, or professional, and others are bad, wrong, or unprofessional.

But because we don't all have the same past experiences, we aren't all making the same decisions and judgments in our unconscious minds.

From Contraction to Expansion

What did I focus on in the situation with my mother-in-law?

Like most of us when we're in an interaction that doesn't go well or our expectations aren't met, I focused on what the other person did. *She went to Miguel instead of talking to me.*

That's the Frame, the external, visible action that's easy to see.

Then my Filters took over and explained and evaluated that behavior, attaching it as a holistic label to her. *She was rude. She was so disrespectful. What a gossiper.* Then those Filters decided what my behavior would be. *I'm going to be respectful (and correct!) and wait for her to come talk to me about the spaghetti.*

My Filters led me to believe that my behaviors were good, the *right* way to approach the situation, and that hers were the *wrong* way.

For both of us, our behavior was the product of a process driven by our Filters. To better understand that, we need to move to use the Active Conscious process.

Remember the Active Conscious graphic? (See figure 4.2.)

Had I used this process, I would have stopped or at least slowed down to challenge those automatic judgments of both her behavior and my own. If I had challenged them, I also needed to be conscious of the intent versus impact dynamic.

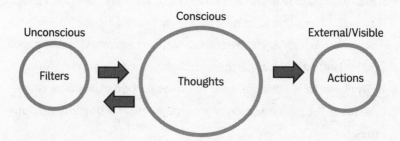

Figure 4.2 Active Conscious Process

Suspend Yours and Focus on Theirs

It is all too common. When an interaction doesn't go well, as for me with my misunderstanding with Esmeralda, what do we typically focus on? Our intent. Which comes from where? Our Filters.

> I was *right*.
> I *didn't mean to hurt you*.
> I was only *being respectful*.

We can even go as far as blaming the other individual for the impact of our actions.

> *You* didn't behave the way you are supposed to.
> *You're* just too sensitive.
> *You* took it the wrong way.

Until we're able to see the full power of our Filters, we have a very limited ability to accept accountability for the negative impact of our actions because we keep listening to the messages from our Filters telling us that what we did was good and came from positive intent. We therefore make the false assumption that our positive intent can only lead to an equally positive impact.

Again, from *Filter Shift*:

> I may have the best of intentions when I have a conversation with you, but if I say something that doesn't sit right with you, well, *you* are the one who ultimately decides on the impact of what I've said, not me.
>
> I might not mean to hurt you, but if I accidentally step on your toe with my stilettos, *you* are the one who decides if it was

painful or not. That's easier to understand when it's physical pain, but the same concept holds true for emotional pain, or joy for that matter.

Our Filters are formed by our personal experiences. They determine how we perceive **through explanations and evaluations**. Because you obviously haven't all had the same experiences I have had, we're not using the same Filters, which means you and I perceive the *same information* differently.

To hold the Filters of others as equally valid, we need to first consider the possibility that our intent wasn't met with an equally positive impact and then shift our focus of positive intent from us and our behavior to them and theirs.

Had I done that with Esmeralda, I wouldn't have immediately jumped to thinking she was disrespectful.

If I consider their behaviors as originating in positive intent, then I can't attach negative evaluations to them. Rude and disrespectful plainly don't stick.

When operating in the stages of lower effectiveness on the left side of the developmental continuum (see figure 4.1), our Filters choose our responses with a goal of being right, good, or respectful. When we operate on the right side, we understand that it's not about being right, good, or respectful but about being *more effective*.

On the left side, it's our Filters that decide how we respond. Because that decision-making process happens unconsciously, we aren't aware that there are other options. Acknowledging that our Filters make decisions for us allows us to consider other possibilities—both in how we could see and experience the situation and how others might be seeing and experiencing it.

Think Twice

Until we have a good sense of Filters, it can be difficult to identify them in any given interaction. They reside in our unconscious, and we can't just open a door into the unconscious to examine our Filters. But what we can do is use the Active Conscious process to think twice about a specific type of thought our Filters create. That specific thought is our expectations, particularly our expectations of the behavior of others.

Keep in mind, we want to identify the objective behaviors, not the value statements coming from our Filters about those behaviors. As an example, the behavior I expected from Esmeralda was face-to-face, direct communication. The value statements coming from my Filters would be respectful communication, or productive communication, even effective communication.

She would have likely used those same positive value statements to describe her completely opposite behavior of indirect communication.

So, in these situations, I do an activity to help me understand my expectations. I list everything I expected on one side and all my descriptors of the other person and their behavior (Esmeralda's, in this instance) on the other side, as indicated in figure 4.3.

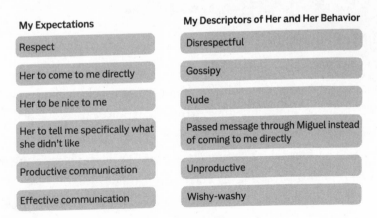

My Expectations

Respect

Her to come to me directly

Her to be nice to me

Her to tell me specifically what she didn't like

Productive communication

Effective communication

My Descriptors of Her and Her Behavior

Disrespectful

Gossipy

Rude

Passed message through Miguel instead of coming to me directly

Unproductive

Wishy-washy

Figure 4.3   Expectations Activity

Then, I look at both lists of descriptors and identify which of them stopped at the first level of See: objective, without judgment. There are only three, which I've highlighted:

- Her to come to me directly
- Her to tell me specifically
- Passed message through Miguel

All the rest are explanations and evaluations—judgments made by my Filters.

Notice how the Filter judgments of my expectations are positive and the Filter judgments of hers are negative.

Next, I assume positive intent on her part. If she had positive intent, then none of my Filter descriptions of her can be accurate. I look at the Filter descriptions of my behavior and assume she had those same positive Filter descriptions attached to her very different behavior. She saw the indirect communication as respectful and productive.

In many ways, then, my Filter judgments, while incredibly strong, are also superfluous. So, I shift them to focus only on the objective information. I'm a direct communicator, and she's an indirect communicator.

Intentionality

One of the most wonderful things about my work is that I have the frequent opportunity to witness development in action in our deep-SEE training programs. This Active Conscious process and new awareness of the participants' Filters is something they are typically amazed by. I often hear comments such as, "I've never been aware of them, but now I'm seeing my Filters all the time!"

That conscious awareness of our Filters is what allows us to acknowledge them, hold them in check, and shift them when necessary.

I often joke with people in our developmental process that you have to *think about what you're thinking about as you're thinking about it and then think about what made you think about what you're thinking about as you're thinking it.*

Instead of skipping over the conscious thought, I visualize it as going back and forth, back and forth, back and forth again between the explanations and evaluations that our Filters send to our conscious mind and checking them over and over again.

That's a lot to hold in our conscious mind, and it can be incredibly awkward as we begin to test out this new way of thinking. The extra thinking takes time and can leave us with blank-stare responses while in interactions as we internally process and check what would normally go unchecked.

Know that the initial awkwardness is normal, and know that you can always put a figurative pin in the situation, respond as you normally would, and then later activate your conscious thinking to go back and forth to check your Filters.

Yes, it's a lot of work. Yes, it takes intentionality and can be exhausting. But going back to the example with my mother-in-law, do I want my Filters to be in control? Do I want to stay locked in a Filter fight with her?

There is often resistance to taking accountability for our own Filters and thus our own behaviors driven by those Filters. Resistance to shifting our Filters and thus shifting our behaviors. It can feel as if we're giving up our own values or giving in to the other person's preferences.

The reality is, it's not *giving up* but *adding on*. Adding new perceptions and thus new behaviors. Had I seen Esmeralda's Filter that associated indirect communication with respect and understood that her Filters were telling her the respectful way to communicate about my spaghetti was through Miguel, then there would have been no Filter fight in the first place!

I wouldn't have *given up* my preference for direct communication, but I also would have had more pleasant interactions with her and would have gained more happiness for *me* in those interactions. That's pure *add-on*.

Keep in mind that the alternative is to continue to be controlled by our Filters, falling into Filter fights with our behaviors completely misinterpreted as coming from negative intent, an alternative I don't think any of us want.

Reflection and Action

- Think back to the behaviors you identified that tend to bother you, those behaviors that you immediately think are rude or disrespectful. Now, consider the intent versus impact in the situation. The behavior obviously elicits a negative impact on you, but can you consider the possibility that it came from positive intent? List out those pet-peeve behaviors, and then next to them, list the potential positive intent that could be driving them.
  - What's important to distinguish is behavior driven by our Filters versus behaviors driven by a stage of development, particularly the second stage. That's the stage where there can actually be the intent to create division, hatred, and even violence.
- Over the next few days, be hyperaware of your Filters using the Active Conscious process. As mentioned, it may be awkward at first, and it also may be distracting. So, if it's easier, instead of using the Active Conscious process in the moment, take time at the end of the day to process the situations you were in, put a pin in the situations that didn't go well or the situations where you expected different behaviors or responses from others. Go back to them when you have time to reflect and engage the Active Conscious process in retrospect.

CHAPTER 5

THE US/THEM AND GOOD/BAD MINDSET

So, who is ready to start identifying their Filters? Those who've developed to the third stage and focus on similarities. The tools of Active Conscious and the SEE model are the homework for starting in that stage and continuing through the remaining stages.

So, what about those who aren't ready for that third-stage homework? What about those who are still in the second stage and focus on surface-level differences? How do we bring them into the developmental process?

We start by understanding the behaviors of this stage for what they are, a reflection of the lack of development.

They're Taking Our Jobs Away

His tense body language of pursed lips, crossed arms, and raised eyebrow were accompanied by periodic sighs of disgust, all mixing together to signal to me he was not happy to be in the training session, and definitely not agreeing with the topic at hand—diversity in the workplace.

Mark was working in a small town that his White family had been a part of for generations, and he was now experiencing what none of his ancestors had experienced: people who didn't look like them moving into the community.

They were moving into his organization, too.

In this case, *they* were immigrants principally from Mexico. Mark's organization, committed to reflecting their community, was becoming more diverse, and Mark now had a Mexican immigrant on his team.

The energy evident in his body language was contained for the first hour or so until he finally let it go.

"They're taking our jobs away! Ya know, HR is even telling us we *have* to hire them. What does this mean for my kids? They aren't ever going to be able to get a job here because they're White."

I knew his statements were hyperbole. I knew they were fueled by his perspective from the second stage of development, a judgmental focus on differences, so he was focusing on differences in Frames and judging those differences. I was fairly certain his statements were rooted in fear and weren't true. Yet I responded by taking him at his word.

"This is serious," I said. "Taking someone's job away—essentially firing them—because of their race is illegal. And hiring someone just because of their race is also illegal. You essentially just reported illegal activity in the organization, and so we're going to need to pause the training to address that."

It wasn't the response he was expecting, as evidenced by his stammering and backtracking.

"Well, I don't mean actually taking our jobs away . . . but, ya know . . . it's just not fair anymore."

Mark was expressing the telltale signs of the mindset of the second stage of development: the judgmental us/them and good/bad dynamic. And for Mark, as is common, this mindset was fueled by fear.

A Focus on Frames

If we've only developed to this level, we're oblivious to our Filters. Our experience of difference is only what we're conscious of: Frames. And our focus is to judge and divide based on those Frames. The polarization that we witness in interactions or in society as a whole is reflective of this judgmental second stage. In fact, one of the cultural competence models names this stage Polarization.[1]

Because we are oblivious to our Filters, they have complete control, which leads us to miss the complexity of situations. We make instant, *subjective* judgments of what's right or wrong. This happens so regularly and so quickly that we accept these judgments as *objectively* true and then attach them globally to entire groups. We look at a tree, and our Filters show us a forest of judgments.

Think of it as a balance scale where we put *us* on one side and *them* on the other. Because there is also a good/bad dynamic, one side of the scale is up, and the group on that side is seen more positively, while the other side is down, and that group is seen more negatively.

Operating in only the second of six stages of competence is not a characteristic of the right or the left, of White or Black, male or female. This is equal opportunity incompetence.[2]

And it is an incompetence that feeds itself because an action from polarization tends to elicit an equal and opposite reaction from polarization. Tell me my group is bad or less than, and the typical reaction is to fight against that or react by telling you how your group is bad or less than.

People who have only developed to this stage with a good/bad focus on differences can be very firm and adamant in their beliefs and judgment.

Where does that knowing and belief come from? It definitely doesn't come from a consciously identified, shared-by-all, agreed-by-everyone database. Instead, it comes from our individual Filters and the inability to challenge them.

We know that in any stage, stereotypes can enter our unconscious without our knowing. But if we have only developed to the second and judgmental stage, we are more likely to *knowingly* take in stereotypical information and *consciously* validate, justify, and reinforce it.

Here are some typical behaviors and beliefs in this second stage:

- Denigration of other groups
- Superiority of my group
- Significant distrust and dislike of other groups
- Pointing out how the other is wrong or bad
- Defending me and mine
- For dominant groups:
  - Claims of reverse discrimination
  - Resistance to "political correctness," which can be evident in the third stage
  - Fear of losing advantage
- For nondominant groups:
  - Defense of my group
  - Distancing from and distrust of other groups

Fear

Of the six stages, this second stage is the only stage that can be coupled with one consistent emotion: fear.[3] Dial up fear, and you're dialing up this second stage. Dial up this stage, and what do you get but more of this stage—a hypersense of this stage. Reduce it and calm fears, and you're better able to advance from this judgmental stage.

I once saw a magic trick that used a magnet on the underside of a table to randomly and suddenly jerk around the objects on top of the table. Those of us watching the trick were distracted by the magician and by the objects moving around the table. We looked for a pattern, naively thinking there would be a logic to the next movement, unaware of the pull of the magnet. Fear is that magnet, hidden from plain view, that pulls us to polarization, causing us to shift our perspective of the other as one we need to defend against or even fight against. Those people and situations that stoke fear, then, like the magician, not only distract us but pull us into this polarizing mindset.

Fear allows our unconscious brain to override the conscious brain in order to make quick judgments. It's the way we have been primitively wired. See tiger. Run. We don't stop to hold a committee meeting to come to consensus on next steps. It's how we make potentially irrational decisions, and that includes the decisions we make about others (the objects of our fear) as well.

Where we direct our fear becomes our *apart-from*, becomes the others that we polarize against, fight against. Those who share that fear and join us in the fight become the *apart-of*.

The increasing acts of hate and violence we're all experiencing are symptoms stemming from increased polarization and anger, at the root of which is fear. Fear can generate anger, and anger can generate violence.[4] While many emotions can lead to violence, such as jealousy, envy, or greed, researchers have found that the principal emotion that leads to violence is anger.

That fear, however powerful, is not discerning and is rudderless, oftentimes steering anger in the wrong direction.

During the COVID-19 pandemic, fear was justifiably on the rise as sickness and death continued to mount. Paralleling the rise of fear was a rise in gun sales, with an 85 percent increase in sales during March 2020 compared with March 2019.[5]

One gun store owner at the time explained the increase: "In the event the outbreak gets worse and civil unrest breaks out, wanting to protect their family and their stockpile is really the vibe we're getting from people."[6] A customer purchasing a gun for the first time explained his purchase: "I don't expect my neighbor to attack me, but if I have to protect my family, I want to be able to."[7]

The fear during the pandemic was real, yet the directionality of that fear was misplaced on the other. As more people were buying guns to protect themselves, crime was actually declining in major cities across the United States.[8] That same March, the epicenter of the pandemic was New York City. During the peak of their pandemic, the last two weeks of March, crime was nearly 20 percent less than the same two-week period in 2019.[9]

It's Still Judgment

"All of X group are lazy!" That's pretty easy to identify as polarization. It's a broad-brushstroke judgment of a full group and every individual in it.

But what if that statement is said by someone *within* X group?

- What if it's another woman claiming that women aren't strategic?
- What if it's another Black person saying other Blacks are lazy and just need to pull themselves up by their bootstraps like they did?
- What if it's another White person claiming all Whites are racists?
- What if it's another man saying all men are clueless?

We easily think about polarization in a way that makes sense—negative judgment is turned outward to the other: us = good; them = bad.

What is misleading is when that judgment is turned inward, and we join forces with the other in their judgment of our own group.

If I as a White person said, "Oh, I so love Hmong family values. I went to the park this weekend and saw 50 of them together, all generations. But then look around and White folks are by themselves, maybe with friends or one or two family members. We Whites have just gotten away from good family values."

Some might call that culturally sensitive or smart, but it's still this second stage that focuses on differences with a broad-brushstroke judgment. I've just turned that judgment inward to my group.

Judge *us* or judge *them*—either way, it's still judgment.

Either way, Filters are left unchallenged.

Being Loud Doesn't Make You Right

Imagine this with our analogy of math again. Let's say we have a classroom of kids trying to figure out a sixth-grade math problem.

It's a long equation, but one of the kids has only a second-grade level of math and seems to not even see the full equation. He only sees the portion of it that is $2 + 2$. He quickly says, "The answer is four!" When he isn't fully acknowledged, he starts to yell it. "THE ANSWER IS FOUR!"

Frustrated at her classmate's ignorance, another student quickly gets into an argument with him, being clear to point out how wrong he is. The second student says the answer is clearly six.

What that second student doesn't realize is that she is wrong too. With only a second-grade level of math herself, she is only seeing another part of the equation, $3 + 3$.

Soon, the argument between the two fills the room and distracts everyone from solving the problem. Others start to question as well. They had different answers, but these two arguing are so vocal, so confident. One set of students shifts their focus from solving the problem to supporting one side or the other of the argument. Another set just gives up, apathetically thinking, "Who cares about this math problem anyway?"

The two in the argument had completely derailed the problem-solving they were all tasked with.

Both were missing parts of the equation. Both thought they were right. What neither of them realized is that with only a second-grade level of math, they couldn't even see what the right answer was.

Unfortunately, this same dynamic happens all too often in conversations and work to advance DEI. Surprisingly, from both sides of the argument, the vocal voices are developed only to polarization and are thus a distraction from solving the whole problem.

Think about polarization—good/bad, us/them—in terms of race, and it's easy to conjure up an image of a skinhead or a member of the KKK. These are the extremes, with individuals such as Robert Bowers believing that White is a supreme race, under threat by Jews and people of color. Whites = us = good; Jews and people of color = them = bad.

Not only is it easy to see that the stage of development of a racist is the judgmental focus on difference of polarization, it's also obvious how they're controlled by their Filters with very black-and-white perceptions of both Black and White.

It's also easy to, well, judge this image of a racist. How could they not realize that they are controlled by their Filters? How could they not realize that they are judgmental and polarizing? Is it honestly fun for them to live in the world of judgment their perceptions have created?

If racists are in the stage of Polarization, controlled by their Filters, then all anti-racists are in anti-Polarization, adeptly checking their Filters, right?

Oh, if it were only that easy.

The added complexity of much of today's DEI work is that it can come from the place of judgmental polarization fueled by Filters.

When It's Performative

"Wait a second. That's the second stage of judgment and division?" As the CEO of a mid-size mission-driven organization, Patricia was referring to a behavior related to DEI work that had become familiar to her. At this point, she had been through most of our deepSEE cultural competence development process and was very familiar with the stages of development. I could see the "aha" moment as it happened for her during one of our training sessions—her eyebrows raised and her mouth dropped slightly open.

The behavior Patricia was referring to is what I call Performative Polarization. It comes from people who are in the dominant group and sincerely want to create equity in their organization, yet have only developed to the judgmental, polarizing stage. These people see this work as a fight and see themselves as righteous warriors, even fighting with others who are working to advance equity to prove that *they* are the ones that *get it*.

This isn't a dynamic unique to Patricia's organization—it has become all too common in a variety of organizations and across communities. At deepSEE, we saw it on the rise after George Floyd's murder, particularly from White staff across organizations. While most prevalent across differences in race, it's not limited to just that difference in identity.

As DEI practitioners, we've become familiar over the decades with the polarizing voice that can come from some in the dominant group who fight because they fear that they will be losing out on something (remember, there are lots of dominant groups depending on the context). We've also become familiar with the equal and opposite response from nondominant groups that are defending against attacks, inequity, or injustice perpetuated against their group.

This performative polarizing behavior is easily misunderstood because it comes cloaked in a desire for greater equity. This leads many, like this CEO, to assume that the behavior is necessary to achieve inclusion and equity.

Here are some examples of the Performative Polarization mindset:

- There's a good and a bad, and if I continually point out how you are bad, then I can't be bad.
- If I point out how you're racist (sexist, ableist, homophobic, etc.) or clueless, that proves I'm not.
- If I shove the data showing inequities of your organization in your face, then I'm the hero for equity.
- You're going to mess up and I'm here ready to pounce when you do.
- I'm on the search for the "gotcha" moment, expecting, even hoping, that someone, anyone, will mess up and I can then be the first to pounce, the first to highlight evidence of that person's cluelessness or their racism, sexism, ableism, or any-ism.

Like the second grader, they lack the ability to solve the problem at hand. For those with Performative Polarization, they are focused only on the surface-level good/bad judgments. They may be loud, but they also distract from the work needed to solve the problem.

Reflection and Action

Over the next few days, watch for examples of Polarization, and remind yourself that regardless of who is making the judgment or whether you agree with them, it's still coming from this developmental stage. The more you can recognize it as developmental, the more you'll be able to respond developmentally (which is what chapter 6 is all about!).

CHAPTER 6

BREAKING THROUGH POLARIZATION

If we have developed to the second stage of development, we tend to focus on differences in Frames and judge those. That's not an effective stage at all. But the good news is that we don't have to stay in this stage. We have a choice to move to more developed and effective stages.

Remember that these stages are developmental, and just as the infant has to develop through the stage of being a toddler before they can develop to the stage of kindergartner, this stage also needs to develop through the last of the ineffective stages before developing into the effective stages. They also have to develop even before they are ready to use the tools of the Active Conscious process or the SEE model.

Those tools are the homework the next stage of development is ready for. This second stage needs a stepping stool of sorts before one can start using those tools. That stepping stool is the development specific to this second stage, which is essentially to start practicing the mindset of that third stage. That is, to start looking for commonality.

What Would a Good Teacher Do?

Think back to the example in the previous chapter of the two second graders with the wrong answers derailing the whole classroom as it worked to solve an equation. In that situation, what would a good teacher do?

It seems obvious, right?

A good teacher would stop the derailment and get the class focused on the actual equation. Most importantly, they would help those two "second graders" learn math.

They'd give them second-grade math homework.

This is our world today. The complex problems of interpersonal misunderstandings and significant societal inequities are the problems we're trying to solve. The complexity of those problems requires that fifth-stage ability to solve.

Few of us have that ability, so it's easy to get distracted by the loud voices of the second graders arguing with each other, not realizing that neither of them has the right answer and that they are consuming the classroom and distracting us from finding the solutions.

The bad news is that folks who have only developed to this stage aren't even ready for the first step of Filter Shift. Ask them to SEE Self, and they will not look to the complexity of their Filters, only to their Frames. Give them information about the validity of others' perspectives, and they will only double down on the validity of theirs.

What's Their Homework?

Remember the balance scale image of Polarization with us on one side and them on the other? The scale is out of equilibrium with one side up, or good, and one side down, or bad.

The homework for this stage is to equalize that balance scale, and the best way to do that is by focusing on commonalities or similarities. Finding similarity with the other helps us lessen the judgment of them.

Come Out from Your Corners

It was as if we were in the middle of a boxing ring. The opponents had gone to their corners, ready for the fight as soon as we referees opened the floor. It was the early '90s, and I was working in Worthington, a small city of 10,000 at the time, tucked into the corner of rural Minnesota. The community was undergoing a significant transformation with an influx of immigrants from across the globe, pulled into the area by the local meat processing plant that had recently deunionized.

In a community that small, the stories easily circulated, stories of immigrants continually stopped by police for no apparent reason, facing discrimination in the workplace and glares and slurs in public. The polarization was palpable.

Now my cofacilitator and I sat in the middle of that polarization in a room with a group of leaders from each of the separate communities. The leaders from the Asian community were in one corner, the African community in another, Latinos in the third, and Whites in the last corner.

I was young in my career and green in my experience, so thankfully my mentor at the time, Juan Moreno, was my cofacilitator. Neither of us was familiar with the developmental model at the time, so it was thanks to either good luck or Juan's experience that our opening activity with the group was developmental.

In the early '90s, the year 2020 felt like a distant future, and we had them focus there. We called the activity 2020 foresight and asked them what kind of community they wanted Worthington to be in that future. Each corner discussed the question and had a reporter share with the large group. As those reports started to unfold, it was soon clear that all the groups agreed.

Regardless of which corner they sat in, they all wanted a community that was safe, with good jobs and where their kids could get a good education. The tension unraveled as they looked across the room and saw people they had commonality with.

Finding Commonality

Let's look at more examples of areas where we can find commonality:

- **Politics:** Start with what we can agree on. It may be the problem, the solution, or even just a common frustration.
- **Family and friends:** Instead of avoiding Thanksgiving dinner because you've seen the polarizing messages your family member has posted and you don't want that to be a part of the conversation, steer the conversation to something you both agree on or have in common. Maybe it's parenting, maybe pets or sports, even the weather. Pick as trivial or meaningful of a topic as you like; just make sure it's a topic you have in common. Even if you pick a polarizing topic, start with a statement or concept that you know you both agree with: *We both agree we're all humans and deserve respect and safety, right?*
- Some quick starter comments:
  - We all want what's best for this situation . . .
  - We're all one human race . . .
  - We both want a respectful workplace . . .
  - This is difficult for all of us . . .
  - I'm a mother too . . .
  - Don't we want a safe community for everyone?

Don't Do This!

I see it all too often. People throw information at the other. It's the individual trying to convince a family member that their polarized view is wrong by listing all the statistics, data, or pundit views that prove them wrong. It's also the organization responding to claims that they are racist by giving a list of all the things they've done that would suggest otherwise.

I even frequently hear people offer that the solution for the political divide is to have those who typically watch CNN watch FOX and vice versa.

It's a natural response to think the problem is just that the other is missing information you happen to have. But giving more or new information causes someone who has developed only to Polarization to further entrench themselves in their views.

As Milton Bennett, the creator of the first cultural competence model, says, this second stage "is a stage of development, not an isolated act." It's "relatively worthless to address the inaccurate assumptions without also addressing" the stage of development. The culprit, as he says, is the lower stage of development, not misinformation.[1]

It Starts at the Top

The role of leaders is critical. In all the thousands of groups and organizations that we've worked with at deepSEE, I have never experienced an organization that operates at a higher stage of development than its leaders. That's not because leaders are somehow better, smarter, or naturally more capable.

It's because leaders set the ceiling and create the culture.

Even if individuals within the organization have developed to a more effective stage, they don't operate at that full potential when they are in a culture that doesn't support it.

The same is true for our country. Bias that resides on a more unconscious level is voiced at a conscious level and legitimized by those in highest power from a place of lowest competence—legitimized through superficial, judgmental sound bites.

To break through polarization, our leaders need to move away from the judgmental good/bad characterizations and lean into and search for the complexity that lies in each group and situation. They need to learn to Filter Shift.

Leaders can also address and reduce Polarization's emotional driver of fear, allaying fear instead of stoking it and looking for connection and hope.

Resistance Is Optional

"So, you're telling me I have to give up my values? No way! I won't do it!"

It's a sentiment I hear frequently from people who have only developed to this judgmental second stage. It makes sense because they feel as if it's a process of giving up versus adding on.

I usually respond to them with an analogy of fixing a kitchen sink. Similar to the first three stages of development, which lack complexity and limit the person to very few options for how to respond, in this analogy, the do-it-yourselfer has only a screwdriver, hammer, and roll of duct tape to fix the sink.

In the latter two stages, we have so many more options for addressing the problem. It's like the contractor who shows up with a van full of hundreds of tools. They still have their screwdriver, hammer, and duct tape, like the do-it-yourselfer. No one has taken those away. But they also know that using any of those tools isn't going to help them fix the sink.

Development is optional. That means that choosing to stay in the judgmental stage is also optional.

Reflection and Action

Go back to the examples of polarization that you identified in the last chapter. Take some time to think about developmental responses that could have pulled the conversation or situation out of this second stage of development.

CHAPTER 7

THE QUAGMIRE STAGE
Where We Get Stuck and How to Keep Moving

Why are nearly 70 percent of us stuck in the third stage,[1] oblivious to our Filters focusing on similarities? If it's 70 percent, does that include you? Chances are it does.

To develop from the third and last of the ineffective stages, we need to first understand why so many of us get stuck there. We also need to recognize what this stage looks like so we can better understand how to develop beyond it.

Am I Being Pranked?

It didn't matter that I had just been on stage as the expert. It also didn't matter that the subject of the conversation afterward was my expertise and not his.

I had been working with an organization for several months, consulting with their internal DEI practitioner and doing cultural competence development with their executive team. The work was so well received, they wanted to introduce it to the board to begin the same development work with them.

Presenting and doing development work in person with a group always jazzes me, and this particular afternoon was no different. The board was engaged and asking great questions, and I could see their "aha" moments as the presentation sparked new connections for them. So, I was riding on that high when I joined them for dinner in the beautiful atrium of their building afterward.

The table was a mix of the organization's senior executives and board members. John, a CEO from a Fortune 100 company and member of the board, said he wanted to sit next to me because he had so many questions he wanted to ask. So he proceeded, through each of the courses, to ask questions related to cultural competence and DEI in organizations.

Yet question after question, he interrupted my response to interject his answer to the question. The only time he listened to a full response was when it came from one of the other male CEOs sitting close by.

It didn't take me long to recognize the pattern of being disregarded and talked over. Worse yet, his comments oozed with the lack of development of the third stage and exposed his complete lack of understanding of the practice of DEI, yet he continued to instruct me, the one with over 30 years of experience in the field.

By the time the main course was served, I had shifted to the *half-in* state, with half of me consciously taking in only enough of the conversation to be able to respond while the other half consciously calculated my options.

My first thought was, "Is this a joke? Am I being pranked?"

The topic of the day and the dinner was DEI, and John, with no DEI experience, thought he had to teach me, the expert. And it wasn't just me. It was obvious that he was dismissing the other women at the table—both CEOs and executive staff—as he also ignored their contributions to the conversation and listened only to the other male CEO as well as to Jack, the organization's CFO.

In my half-in state, I remembered the mental exercise one of my former colleagues would do in similar situations: solve for *x*, with *x* being the reason for his behavior.

That is, while it seemed obvious that he was treating me differently because I was a woman, I wanted to give him the benefit of the doubt and consider other possibilities. Could there be some other unknown reason I hadn't considered?

I do this exercise frequently as an Active Conscious exercise. It might be with a client at work or a cashier at the store. Either way, I'm challenging the first explanation my Filters give for their behavior that doesn't sit well with me for whatever reason.

Could they be having a bad day?
Could this be because of something happening in a different context in their life?
Do they treat everyone this way?
Is this just an isolated instance?

In the case of John, solving for *x* had me asking a couple of questions:

Could it be because of an age difference?
   The answer to that was no because we were relatively the same age.
Could it be because I'm not a CEO of a Fortune 100 company, and he only respects the perspective of other CEOs of large organizations?
   The answer to that was clearly no because he was listening to Jack, the CFO, and not listening to the other CEOs, who were women.

The reason for his behavior toward me, the *x* I was left with, was that I was a woman.

I knew what my options were. After all, I teach this stuff every day. I could *fight* and call him out on his behavior, maybe even frame it as a teaching moment. Just getting up and leaving in *flight* was another option, which I knew I wasn't going to take. Nor would I take the third option, *fawn*, by praising him for his knowledge and insight, of which I could find none.

The final option is what I eventually took, which was *freeze*.

In this case, this particular day and situation, I took that option consciously, knowingly.

I was tired after a really long day, and taking the only other viable option of the teaching moment was too much of a fight I didn't want to take on because I didn't trust myself to not verbally punch this guy in the face with an assault of statistics and mirror-in-the-face examples, pointing out how his comments were casebook examples of the third stage and how his behavior was a blatant microaggression.

Instead I stayed in that half-in state for the rest of the meal, continuing to attend the conversation only partially as I nonverbally checked in with the other women at the table. Their widening or rolling eyes confirmed that they saw it too. Yet the men at the table seemed oblivious.

It was clear that the women at that table shared a different experience than the men. The Filters we had accumulated in our lifetimes of working as women leaders in the corporate world had exposed us to this behavior that overlooked and disregarded us before. It was familiar, and we had decades of accumulated Filters to confirm it was real.

"Being in the vicinity of events does not construe experience."[2] Our Filters do.

Did I resolve the situation with the CEO? No. It was a battle that particular day that I chose not to fight because the risks were high and any reward was unlikely. I use the story to illustrate an example of the third stage of development through John's behavior and an example of identity-based experience for the women present.

The Quagmire Stage

John was like most individuals, developed only to the third stage of development. Although he likely had positive intent, he clearly left me, and likely the other women at that table, with a very different, negative impact. John wasn't his most effective in that situation because of his lack of ability to see and challenge his Filters.

And he was completely unaware.

People who have developed to this third stage, like John, have moved beyond the conscious judging of the previous, polarizing stage, yet their Filters are still in control.

Why are almost 70 percent of us stuck in this stage?

First, because it's a big developmental leap to move to the next stage. I often describe it as the difference between grade school and grad school. That's because we need to develop from a stage where we're oblivious to our Filters to a stage where we are able to acknowledge our Filters and be aware of them in any given situation.

That's the reason we focus so strongly on Filters as part of the developmental process.

The second reason is because this stage sits between two stages that can be misperceived, one as the other. It's as if we're in a mirage where the stage we would develop to if we escaped from the quagmire appears to be the same stage we just came from. We don't want to go backward, but forward looks like the same thing, so we stay sitting in the quagmire.

The reason they feel or sound the same is because the second and fourth stages have a significant similarity. That is, they both consciously identify and address difference.

Yet the stages are not the same. In the second stage, that acknowledgment of difference is the broad brushstroke that is also judgmental. The fourth stage, on the other hand, acknowledges complexity in
differences and does so without judgment.

Even more significantly, the second stage operates in the land of
Frames, while the fourth stage is able to operate in the land of Filters
as well.

How Does It Manifest?

The placement of this stage developmentally is key. It's sandwiched
between a stage that addresses differences in Frames with judgment
and a stage that addresses differences of Filters without judgment.
Focusing on similarity is the way this stage bridges that gap.

When we have developed to this third stage and are focusing on
similarities, we have gotten beyond seeing other groups as a threat,
and we also avoid outwardly, consciously denigrating or stereotyp-
ing. We're more comfortable not talking about obvious differences
and instead focus on our similarities.

The mindset of this stage is that a focus on differences divides; a
focus on similarity unites. We believe we're more alike than different
and that shared universal values guide us all and help us to resolve
any misunderstanding. What we then miss is the multitude of complex differences.

Our Filters get in the way in this stage by making an unconscious
assumption of similarity. The Golden Rule is an example of this assumption. Do unto others as you would have them do unto you.

That's based on a huge assumption: that the whole world wants
to be treated the way you want to be treated. And it's our Filters that
make that assumption of similarity—based on our own past experiences, of course. Their automatic process just sends explanations and
evaluations to our conscious mind without a disclaimer.

P.S. These thoughts are only based on your experiences and will likely not be relevant or true to the individual you are interacting with.

If we're able to challenge and shift our Filters, we're able to exhibit the Platinum Rule: Do unto others as they would do unto themselves.

Power of the Puppeteer

As with the second stage, our Filters are still in control in this third stage, making this another ineffective stage. What's different is that when we develop to this stage, we move beyond the conscious, blatant judgment, which tricks us into believing we have no judgment at all, leaving us to miss the well of evaluations that spring up from our Filters to dictate our thoughts and behaviors.

Couple that with a focus on our positive intent versus on the impact on others. Put those two together, and we have well-minded individuals who sincerely believe they are respectful and inclusive, completely controlled by their Filters, which at times makes them anything but respectful and inclusive.

Does that sound like John?

And remember, the vast majority of individuals have developed only to this stage.

There's a 70 percent chance that includes you as well, regardless of your identity.

When the breadth and depth of our differences reside in our Filters and the nature of this stage is to pretend differences aren't there, this stage allows our Filters a certain kind of power. We aren't actively challenging them, so they have free rein.

Much like a puppet, John was controlled by that free rein of the puppeteer hidden behind the curtain, his unconscious Filters. As a puppeteer, our Filters are ceded even more power when we pretend they don't exist. Yet tell John about his Filters and how they are controlling him, and I'm sure he would categorically deny that and even be offended.

That's because he needs to become aware of the puppeteer for himself.

The puppeteer of our Filters pulls the strings of our thoughts to create our behaviors. When we're only developed to this stage, we truly are puppets. While we may not be able to see the puppeteer of our Filters because those Filters operate in our unconscious, what we can see, if we look for them, are the strings pulled by our Filters that determine our actions, and those strings are our thoughts.

The expanded consciousness process helps us examine the thoughts for what they are, the connection between our unconscious and our visible actions.

For someone like John, acknowledgment and accountability are key. He may not see the stereotypical bias that likely created his behavior, but if, in general, he acknowledges he has Filters and accepts accountability for them, those strings of the Filter-created thoughts will eventually become more visible.

Development

To develop from this third stage where we focus on similarities, we must be able to **assume difference in Filters without judgment, starting with our own.**

Because our Filters unconsciously assume similarity, to counterbalance that automatic process, we consciously assume difference and look for greater complexity.

This is where the Active Conscious process comes in again. I stop and challenge what my Filters are telling me, especially to challenge that assumption of similarity.

- I am different, not the norm.
- My Filters may be wrong, so I assume different from what my Filters tell me. I challenge my Filters.
- The other person has Filters different from mine, and their behaviors are relative to themselves and their Filters, not mine.

We also need to move away from the judgmental evaluations our Filters make. The best way to do that is to both assume positive intent coming from others as well as to question the impact of our own Filter-driven behaviors. This approach might not make sense. Why do we focus on the positive intent of others when we don't focus on our own positive intent?

Keep in mind that we're not talking here about intentional acts of divisiveness, hatred, or othering. We're talking about misunderstandings, ineffectiveness, and even harm that can be initiated with either benign or positive intent. Think back to my example of the spaghetti with my mother-in-law. We both had positive intent. If I focus only on me and my positive intent as well as the impact she had on me, I'm missing her positive intent and therefore misinterpreting her behavior.

Identity-Based Experience

In this particular situation, as a woman, I was in the nondominant group. It was easy for me and the other women at that table to see that our experience at that dinner was different from the experience for the men, and that experience was based on our identity.

That's when it's easy to see—when we don't fit, when we are in the nondominant group. But when we are in the dominant group, like the men at the table, it's often difficult to see past the Filters of our own experience, especially if we haven't developed past the third stage.

Keep in mind, dominant groups aren't just based on gender and race. Each one of us is in situations when we are in the dominant group, whether because of our age, role, religion, education, position in a family, and so on. Having said that, some of us have that opportunity much more often.

Being in the dominant group, where the culture matches our culture, tends to lead to not only advantage but also *conscious laziness*. We are easily unaware of the different experiences others are having because of their identity, and it is our Filters that are mostly to blame.

Our Filters Care Only about Our Own Past Experiences

Even though our Filters are taking in 11 million pieces of information every second, their warehouse of information is incredibly limited because it is a vacuum of only our own past experiences. Even if our own past experiences aren't important, relevant, or even right, the job of our Filters is to link them to our current situation. It's a job they take very seriously.

I recently witnessed my own Filters in action in this regard. Romy, my sister-in-law, was telling me she hadn't slept well and that she woke up with a lot of pain in her knee because she had forgotten to sleep with a pillow between her knees as she typically does.

After she told me, did I empathize? Did I tell her how sorry I was that she didn't sleep well or that her knee was hurting?

Nope.

Instead, my Filters immediately took me straight to my own past experiences. I reminded her about the multiple surgeries I've had on my knee. Then I told her the story about how, after the first surgery, when I was finally off a mobility machine, the nurses in the hospital always put a pillow between my knees. That was over 30 years ago, and I'm still sleeping with a pillow between my knees.

All of that . . . *my* surgeries, *my* experience in the hospital, the nurses tending to *my* knee and *my* habit of using a pillow . . . *my* experiences. That's where my Filters took me.

In response to her telling me about *her* bad night's sleep, I relayed all *my* experiences. I'm embarrassed to say that I was in the middle of it all before I realized I didn't even acknowledge her current situation, just my past experiences.

I know I'm not the only one to do this because I see others do it all the time:

- The person who doesn't acknowledge their coworker's story about being sick but instead launches into their own story about when they were sick a month ago
- The parent who tells all about the system they created years ago to chauffeur their kids to soccer practice instead of acknowledging the statement just made by another parent about how difficult the chauffeuring routine is for them with their kids right now
- The friend who launches into all the ways their ex was a jerk instead of acknowledging the pain their friend is going through in a current relationship

We respond to someone else's current reality through the lens of our own past experiences—our Filters.

This is yet another opportunity to practice the Active Conscious process and challenge our Filters. When we pause to put our Filter responses on hold, it allows us to be more present in the moment.

Pausing these Filter responses is also a necessary Active Conscious skill that we need to deploy if we want to understand identity-based experiences.

When something doesn't match our experience, our Filters disregard or invalidate it, judge it negatively, or miss it entirely. Their job isn't to tell us that others have different experiences and therefore different Filters. That Filter reality check can only happen in the conscious mind.

"I had no idea that was happening in the work world until my daughter started working and telling me about her experiences." I've heard quotes like this from men in our programs numerous times. They had been in that same work world for decades and had probably even heard about discrimination, harassment, and microaggressions against women, but it wasn't until someone close to them told them of a different experience that they actually witnessed it and believed it.

That's easy when it comes to gender. Most men have several women in their lives they are close to. When it comes to race, that's not the case. The average White person's network is only 1 percent Black. And it's not much higher for other races either.[3] Without that conscious check from someone we trust, how do we know that their experience is different?

Walking while Black

He was just walking, but it didn't matter; the police continually stopped him anyway. Six feet two, over 200 pounds, 17 years old, and Black. While in high school, our second son, Gabriel, found a job at Burger King just a half mile away, which meant he could walk to work. And that was the option he frequently chose because he had to pay for his own gas if he was using the car.

It would happen several times in just a matter of weeks. He would get stopped by the police while walking to or from work, questioned about where he was going, where he lived, and why he was walking at that place and time.

I lived in that same neighborhood for 21 years and walked several times each week. On the same streets he couldn't get past without the police stopping to question him, I was only greeted with smiles and friendly nods by other pedestrians. In all of my 21 years there, I was never once stopped by the police while walking.

Our experiences are based on our identities.

Why would that matter? Why do we need to know this, and what do our Filters have to do with it?

To reach an end goal of reducing systemic inequities, we need to fully acknowledge the reality of identity-based experiences. Yet if we don't develop beyond this third stage of development, it's unlikely we'll be able to do so.

Reflection and Action

Practice challenging the assumption of similarity with the prompts I mentioned. Think of a person you know well, maybe a coworker, close friend, spouse, or sibling. Then think of one of their behaviors that bothers you.

- What do your Filters tell you about that behavior?
- Now challenge your Filters by assuming something different from what your Filters tell you.
- The other person has Filters different from yours, and their behaviors are relative to them and their Filters, not you and your Filters. Theirs come from positive intent just like yours do.
- Can you understand their behavior relative to their Filters and their experience?

CHAPTER 8

INTENT ISN'T THE POINT
The Filter Harm of Microaggressions

Knowing our Filters and developing the ability to challenge them in order to shift our actions helps us to be more effective. Filters are also the source of microaggressions, a form of identity-based harm. On the path to creating greater equity, we must first ensure we're not perpetuating or causing harm to others. Once again, to do so, we need to know how our Filters drive our thoughts and behaviors.

The Flight Attendant

Even before I could give her a hug and before she loaded her luggage in the car, she was already unloading about the flight attendant.

My daughter Elizabeth was 20 at the time and coming home for Thanksgiving break, and I was so excited to see her, looking forward to the days ahead with her home. But instead of excitement, the baggage she brought off the plane with her was a mix of anger, frustration, and indignation.

The flight was a short one from Chicago to Minneapolis, and she was happy to be sitting in an exit row seat with extra leg room. Happy, that is, until the exchange with the flight attendant.

Sitting next to Elizabeth with the thick, hard dividers of the exit row and a world of different experiences between them sat another young woman. Though the two appeared to have age and college-student status headed home for the holidays in common, their similarities in Frames ended there.

Straight blond hair and White skin, she sat in contrast to Elizabeth.

For as long as she can remember, Elizabeth has fielded the questions, the worst being, "What are you?" From classmates to acquaintances and even Uber drivers and strangers, they have thrown their guesses at her, like surprise-attack daggers hitting her many times with no warning and just as often with a curious smile on the lips of the questioner. Are you Middle Eastern? Brazilian? A hybrid? Or even more brazenly stating versus asking: No, you're Mexican! You're Egyptian!

We had a contest of sorts in our household at the beginning of every school year. What would be the date and who would be the first teacher to ask the question?

Our daughters are incredibly smart and kind. They are the beautiful manifestations of Miguel's Haitian and Dominican lineage along with my Irish and Scandinavian lineage. They didn't look like the majority White kids in their school, but they also didn't look like the Black kids or the Latine kids who were mostly from Mexico and Central America. So, unfortunately, they were accustomed to the question of our yearly contest, "Where are you from?"

With olive skin, a broad, freckle-streaked nose, and a halo of thick, curly, black hair, Elizabeth learned to answer from a very young age with, "Well, I'm from Woodbury, but I don't think you're asking about where I live. I think you're asking why I look like I do. It's because my dad is Black, and my mom is White."

On this particular flight, it had been all standard practice—the boarding, the announcements, and, of course, the question from the flight attendant to Elizabeth and her fellow exit row occupants.

100   Thinking at the Speed of Bias

"Are you willing and able to perform the duties and functions of the exit row seat?"

It was the young White woman sitting at the window who responded first: "Mm-hmm." With a smile of acknowledgment to the White woman, the flight attendant then turned to Elizabeth in the aisle seat, awaiting her answer. Now sitting next to me in the car, she was still fuming as she relived the experience. "I didn't even think. I don't know why; it just came to me to parrot her, and so I also said, 'mm-hmm.' In the affirmative."

That's when everything shifted, and the pointing finger, raised eyebrows, pursed lips, and stern demeanor of the flight attendant emerged. "I'm going to need a verbal yes or no from you." While their responses had been the same, she only addressed Elizabeth.

"Just yesterday someone was in the exit row, and I let them by when they responded 'mm-hmm' to my question," she told her. "And then, when we did service, we couldn't understand what he was saying, and he couldn't understand what we were saying. He didn't even speak one word of English. Our whole flight was at risk because he couldn't speak English and he was sitting in the exit row. So, as I said, I'm going to need a verbal yes or no!"

Again, only to Elizabeth.

Now might be a good time to mention that while all my children passionately point out injustice when they see it, Elizabeth is the emotionally expressive extrovert who shouts that injustice from any platform every chance she gets. When she was only 12, she was meeting with her legislators to lobby for marriage equity. She chose the career of law so she could work to right injustice in the world. In any conversation about disparity, her voice and passion for the rights of those marginalized is always clear, strong, and loud.

So, I have to admit that my first thought as she was telling me this story, now sitting safely in the car with me, was, *Okay, she came out of*

*the airport on time, so I'm guessing no flight marshals were involved in
whatever came next.*

That's because she also learned from an early age when to shout,
when to teach, and when shouting and teaching won't sink in or make
a difference, and thus, when to let it pass. "What I really wanted to say
was, 'What language do you want it in, because I can respond in
English, French, Spanish, or Xhosa?" She said this to me with all the
justified aggravation and indignation I know she would have wanted
to respond to the flight attendant with.

In the moment, however, her response was just a restrained, "Yes."

Along with the injustice of this story, there is an incredible irony.
The flight attendant was adamant as she questioned Elizabeth, for
the purpose—as she said herself—of safety. Yet to this day, we don't
know if that flight was safe. Why?

Because we don't know if the White woman sitting next to Elizabeth spoke English.

Filter Harm

It wasn't that flight attendant but rather her Filters that were in control, making associations, shaping and justifying her behavior. But if
our Filters are wrong or biased, the behavior they justify will be
equally as tainted and ineffective and may even harm the other individual.

The behavior stemming from biased Filters can harm others in
the form of microaggressions.

The concept and term of *microaggressions*, originally conceived
by Chester Pierce of Harvard nearly five decades ago, have entered the
common vernacular.[1] Writings outline typical examples,[2,3,4] and different professions and organizations have sought to detail responses
to and interventions for those impacted.[5,6,7] Yet to stop ourselves
from committing them, we need to understand their origins and

specifically, the four distinct ways our Filters can create offensive or even harmful behavior if we aren't aware.

Microaggressions

First, let's define what it is we're talking about.

Microaggressions are identity-based, stereotypical statements or actions that appear innocuous or benign on the part of the sender yet have significant or even traumatic short- or long-term impacts on the receiver.

Identity Based

Microaggressions are the outward manifestations of Systemic Filters. As we know, the initial source of all our visible, external behavior is our unconscious Filters. When those are Systemic Filters, the behavior they create aligns with stereotypes. Stereotypes are judgmental and, with a broad brushstroke, obscure any complexities of an entire group of people: "All of X group are smart." "All of Y group are lazy."

Not only do stereotypes not allow for deviation; they also don't allow for complexity. Everyone in Y group is lazy, and there is no other descriptor for the whole group or identity, no other explanation or evaluation.

Because they are identity based, they are also exclusionary. Tiffany Jana, founder and CEO of TMI Consulting and coauthor of *Subtle Acts of Exclusion: How to Understand, Identify, and Stop Microaggressions,* explains: "The behavior might be subtle and not intentional, but it serves to exclude people and pushes them further on the margins."[8]

What microaggressions are *not* is rude or offensive behavior in general. The cashier having a bad day who is rude to everyone or the equal opportunity jerk who creates a cloud around them wherever they go are not examples of microaggressions. They're just examples of bad behavior.

With identity-based trauma, these associations are stereotypical. X group is smart. Y group is lazy. And the freeway has been established with years of experiences taking in movies, TV shows, news clips, social media, memes, and advertisements. The result is that most individuals, as we know, hold stereotypical bias.

Innocuous or Benign Intent on the Part of the Sender

While some people may categorize intentional acts of discrimination, hate, and otherness as microaggressions, this conflation blurs the very different source of these acts versus microaggressions and thus confuses mitigation strategies. Intentional acts of othering are examples of the ineffective second stage of development. As we know, the developmental strategy for the second stage is to seek commonality.

The sender of a microaggression, on the other hand, has either positive or benign intent. The disconnect between that positive intent of the sender and the negative impact on the receiver is even more difficult for the sender to understand because the origins of their behavior lie in their Filters, unconscious to them.

Traumatic Impact on the Receiver

Trauma is a physical response to an emotional event. For centuries, our bodies have evolved, and our automatic reactions have sharpened to respond to threat or danger. For early humans to survive, when the tiger jumped out from behind the bush, the sympathetic nervous system kicked in, increasing the heart rate and sending the body's energies away from internal systems and organs toward extremities to allow fight or flight.[9]

The modern-day version of the tiger are situations such as war, abuse, and physical violence. These more extreme situations are commonly referred to by mental health professionals as *big-T trauma*.[10]

Microaggressions typically fall in the category of *small-t trauma*, day-to-day emotional stresses.[11] While not as immediately life-threatening as the pouncing tiger, they still cause our bodies to respond physically, to quickly, automatically move from the calm parasympathetic state to the heightened, blood-rushing sympathetic state.

Trauma Compounded

Microaggressions, then, end in harm to the receiver yet are facilitated by lack of awareness and competence on the part of the sender. This intent and impact gap not only causes misunderstanding but also distraction from the root cause. So what is the root cause of microaggressions?

Our Filters.

Before we go further, let's go back to the Harvard IAT. It shows us that there are patterns to stereotypes. X group is smart. Y group is lazy. Not the other way around. We also know those patterns of stereotypes come from Systemic Filters.

Those same patterns, then, show up in patterns in the microaggressions along with patterns in the experience of and impact on the receiver.

That means they're not individual, random events without connection.

There are patterns in the stereotypical Filter and patterns even in the kinds of things that are said and done as microaggressions. When a receiver continually experiences the same trauma resulting from the same pattern, it can increase the negative impact. Think about the example with Elizabeth. She's received the impact of the same Filter pattern for decades. That doesn't make it easier to deal with; many times it can compound the impact.

Even if we haven't received it before, just knowing that it's coming from a stereotype can have a compounding effect.

Remember, any of us can find ourselves in the dominant group depending on the situation and the differences at play. While some find themselves in that situation much more often, this is still a lesson for all of us.

It's about Patterns

To ensure we aren't perpetrating microaggressions, we need to understand those patterns of behaviors. To do that, we once again go back to the Filters that created them. There are four specific patterns in our how our Filters operate that help us understand the resulting microaggressions:

- Filter associations
- Lack of associations
- Lack of exposure
- Partial consciousness

Filter Associations

In the case of the flight attendant, the Filter harm was created by a Filter association. Remember the high-speed freeway that connects two things, such as peanut butter and jelly, in our unconscious? The flight attendant's Filters traveled on that high-speed freeway to connect the Frame of Elizabeth's hair, the color of her skin, and her features to the association of non-English speaker. In milliseconds, the explanation and evaluation were made, the decision passed to the flight attendant's conscious mind, and the behavior was set in motion. Knowing that she responded so quickly to Elizabeth, it's likely she may not have been fully aware of that conscious thought. It was just a quick passive step in between her Filter and her actions.

Race and Threat Association

As mentioned, the Harvard IAT shows that most individuals who have taken the test—73 percent, to be specific—associate Black Americans with weapons and White Americans with harmless objects.[12] As we know, Filters manifest in external behaviors whether we consciously agree with those Filters or not. Those behaviors in turn create identity-based experiences that are different across races.

Correlating with this specific IAT result, Black men in particular describe the identity-based trauma of:

- bystanders calling security about them even when they are displaying the same behavior as White people in the same situation;
- women clutching or moving their purse when a Black man enters the room;
- people moving to the other side of the street as if to avoid them; and
- White women taking a different elevator or creating more distance in a shared elevator.

Gender and Race with Career, Leadership, and Competence Association

Knowing that over 90 percent of Fortune 500 CEOs are White men, when a Google search for images of CEOs produces the same demographic and when our movies, TV shows, and history all portray the same, it's easy to understand how 79 percent of individuals associate men with careers and women with home and family (Harvard IAT). If the well-trafficked freeway travels between leader and White male, that leaves the rutted and rarely traveled pathway between leader and BIPOC or leader and woman. The result is a common experience by individuals in those groups of people

- who are continually passed over for opportunities or promotion;
- who are being talked over or ignored in work settings or in personal settings when a partner from the dominant group is present;
- whose idea isn't an idea and isn't even heard until someone outside their group expresses it;
- who do or give 110 percent yet are seen as doing or giving 75 percent;
- who come in to interview for a manager's position and are asked if they are there to fix the copy machine;
- who have the credentials and experience but are told, "Let me explain this for you," by the person from the dominant group who doesn't; and
- who hear statements that insinuate their hire was a result of affirmative action or diversity programs and not their merit:
  - "Yes, we want diversity, but we have to make sure people are capable."
  - "Some people actually had to work to get this position."

Nationality and Language

Identity-based trauma also shows up in relationship to nationality and language, particularly with the association that only Whites and Blacks are from the United States. Asian Americans, Latines, people from the Middle East, and anyone who appears racially ambiguous aren't "from here" and therefore don't speak English, even if they were born and raised in the United States or their family has been in the country for generations. Examples include:

- "You're so articulate," or "You speak so well."
- "Where did you learn your English?"

- "Where are you from?... No, I mean, where are you really from?"
- The sender speaking louder and slower.

Lack of Associations

It's not just the presence of reinforced associations that cause harm—our unconscious creates patterns of behavior when an association is completely absent as well. It's as though the Filters are circling in a parking lot, searching for that freeway entrance. No roads exist in our own minds to connect two points. Therefore, we resist any information that does connect them, and when we're presented with that, we may even argue against it.

The Wedgewood Woman

We were a bit out of our typical routine that summer evening. With our girls in elementary school and our boys already out of the house, our typical routine involved figuring out which parent would take which kid to which soccer field, each parent driving separate directions.

On this particular evening, with just one soccer practice on the calendar, we decided to all go together, first dropping off Elizabeth at the soccer field, then Miguel and I heading to a tennis court with Maria, our younger daughter.

In those years, when my knees could still handle it, Miguel and I played a lot of tennis together. It was a fun way in our busy schedules for us to spend time together and get a workout. While our kids rarely tagged along, this time Maria was excited to join us as we waited for Elizabeth to finish practice.

In those years, we lived in Woodbury, a suburb of St. Paul and a community that was full of parks, where it was always easy to find public tennis courts close by. We had played on several of them, but this one, nestled in Wedgewood, one of the wealthier neighbor-hoods, was new to us. Close to the soccer fields, it seemed like a won-derful find, and we assumed it would be our new staple court for the summer.

Little did we know we'd never want to return thanks to the "Wedge-wood Woman," as we soon came to refer to her.

We started with a game, Maria and I playing doubles against Miguel, but after just a few sets, she got bored. So Miguel, ever the teacher, decided to do drills with her. As he worked with her on her form, I took on ball duty. That's when I saw the Wedgewood Woman approaching in the distance, walking her dog. The park's path circled the court on three sides like a horseshoe, and I saw her approaching next to the long side of the court on the other side of the fence where I was busy retrieving balls.

Before she even reached the fence, she was calling out to me.

"Is he teaching lessons?"

My immediate Filter explanation of her was that she was a grand-mother who needed a tennis coach for her granddaughter. My Filters also immediately decided that she belonged to this wealthy neigh-borhood with her expensive jogging suit, coifed hair, and White skin.

Instead of more explicitly answering her question by saying, "No, he's not a coach," I guess I thought I was still answering the question but with different information by saying, "No, she's our daughter."

The interchange went downhill fast.

"Well, he's teaching lessons, and he can't teach lessons here in a public court."

I recognized it right away. It was a lack of association. She literally couldn't take in the information I was telling her. And for some, you might say, *perverse* reason, I consciously decided to continue giving her the same information to see just how long it would take her Fil-ters to make the association.

I continued volleying the same statement to her, and she continued missing it as she confidently swung her statements back at me.

"No, she's our daughter."

"I know he's teaching lessons, and he can't do that on a public
court."

"No, she's our daughter."

"I used to work at city hall, and he needs to register as a coach and
pay a fee, and I know he hasn't."

By this time, she had reached the portion of the path that ran next
to the end of the court, and Miguel, who had just a moment before
been on the other end of the court, suddenly appeared at my side,
propelled in superhuman speed by his indignation, ready to defend
himself and his family.

While he and I were both responding to her, she only looked at
and listened to me. It took me saying "she's our daughter" four times
before it finally set in, or at least before she moved to a different argument.

As if still needing to protest our presence in some way, she said,
"Well, you're not from Woodbury, so you can't use our public courts."

Why did we respond? Why did we think she even deserved a response? Why did we feel the need to defend?

I don't know, but we both did.

We shot back at her, "Yes, we do live in Woodbury." And then we
even gave her more information than she deserved. "We live in the
Fox Run neighborhood."

As if slapping us with the fact that we didn't live in the wealthy
part of town, she said, "Well, you don't pay as much as we do in taxes,
so you shouldn't use these courts."

Thankfully for all of us, by this time she had reached the portion
of the path that turned away from the courts, and a 10-foot-high
fence between us kept Miguel and me from running after her with

our need to somehow defend ourselves, our need to argue with her and at least figuratively slap her in the face with evidence of her bias.

While she strolled away with her dog, we were left with an overpowering fury and exasperation competing with an equally overpowering need to make sure Maria was okay. Of course, she hadn't physically been hurt, but the Wedgewood Woman had violated our peace and had questioned us as a family. And it had to have been scary for her to see her parents both so immediately and negatively affected by this woman and the interaction.

While the vehemence of the Wedgewood Woman was more extreme, her *lack of associations* is commonplace for Maria and for the rest of us as a family. We just don't "go together" in most people's brains. We can all walk into a restaurant together, and the host will look just to me and ask us if I want a table for one. We walk into establishments together where we have a family membership card that I present for all of us to pass, and then the security stops the rest of my family, asking for their card.

As the Wedgewood Woman strutted with her dog, she also exhibited typical signs of a lack of associations.

First, even though I repeated the same statement several times, she still couldn't take it in. By being closed to that association, she was actually closed to reality and even argued for a counter-reality, her unconscious all along telling her she was right.

While she remained persistent to keep her associations closed to reality, most who have a lack of association eventually take in at least a bit of the new pathway, and the common reactions are surprise or even startlement or acknowledging the reality yet continuing to express disbelief.

- "Can I speak to the person in charge?" said to a young woman who responds, "I am in charge." "I mean the *actual* boss."

- "You mean you're not the nanny?" said to my colleague, a woman of color about her mixed-race kids.
- "You're here on an engineering scholarship? But you have a basketball scholarship too, right?" said to my tall, unathletic Black friend when he was in college.

Lack of Exposure

Although he's lived in the United States for nearly 30 years, it took only a few months for Miguel to see the patterns, patterns in the very few things that people in the United States associate with the DR.

They manifest through what I call the Stupid Question Syndrome. It's what happens when a lack of exposure gives us few, if any, Filters to associate with a group.

While there are a gazillion descriptors, data points, or bits of history that could be used to describe a particular group, with a lack of exposure, most only know a few data points. In Miguel's case, that group is Dominicans and the DR. When it comes to the DR, if the patterns Miguel has seen are any indication, those few things are baseball, beaches, and poverty.

So, of those countless things that are true about and describe him as a Dominican or his country of the DR, he only hears the same (stupid) questions over and over again, reflective of the few Filters Americans tend to have without any real exposure to the DR:

- "Miguel, do you play baseball?" (He does.)
- "Do you know Sammy Sosa?" (He doesn't. And he jokes that he could respond with, "I don't, which is strange because I know every one of the other 11 million Dominicans!")
- "Did you grow up on a beach?" (He didn't.)
- And then there was the stupid and incredibly hurtful question during an interview for a civil engineering position: "In the

DR, do you build with concrete, or is it just, you know, mud or earth and, you know, sticks?"

Partial Consciousness

As we develop, we become more consciously aware of our Filters. Yet until we develop the ability to then shift to a more effective behavior, we circle around in a conscious swirl of acknowledgment, awkwardness, guilt, and overcompensation.

We can acknowledge a lack of exposure or potential Filter associations, but we don't know *how* to respond or even *that* a different response is needed. This shows up in three different ways:

- Stereotype threat
- Belief that acknowledging is enough
- Tokenizing

Stereotype Threat

Initially coined by Claude Steele and Joshua Aronson, the term *stereotype threat* describes a phenomenon researchers found in students asked to take an aptitude test.[13] If they were asked to identify their racial identity prior, they performed differently and more in line with stereotypes. Asians performed better in math than White and Black students, as an example.

This focus was on the individual responding differently because they were unconsciously associating with a stereotype. Since then, the term has expanded to include behaviors by those concerned they may stereotype others. They are consciously aware of the typical Filters yet don't know how to respond effectively, so the response is a less authentic, more awkward one.

- It's the person who interacts for the first time with a colleague who is blind. They consciously worry they will stereotype, worry they will offend, so after they reach out to shake hands and realize the person can't see the gesture, they hypercorrect, jerking their hand back: "It's so great to see you! I mean . . . it's great to, you know, . . . I mean, it's great." Stammering and tripping over themselves the whole time.

- It's the overcompensating colleague who knows some of the Filter associations and bias experienced by LGBTQ+ folks in the workplace and wants to be sure to not perpetuate any of those associations, so they double down on acknowledging the partner: "Make sure to invite John's husband!" "John, is your husband coming?" "John, where is your husband?" "It was so great that your husband could come, John!" All at the same time not acknowledging any of the straight partners.

They are clear of the biased Filter, clueless of the effective behavior.

Acknowledging Is Enough

All too often, those in dominant groups mistakenly believe that acknowledging the Filter association is enough. Once again, they are clear that there is a Filter but clueless of the effective behavior:

- "Well, we don't want to ask Mary, the only woman, to take notes!" said with a chuckle. "Let's make sure one of the guys takes the notes this time!"
- "Some of my best friends are _____."
- Out of the blue, they mention the volunteer work they do with marginalized communities or the racial justice protest they just attended.

Tokenizing

One step further than just acknowledging, though not necessarily more effective, is to then take limited action, particularly through tokenizing:

- The man who sees no women on his leadership team of ten, hires one or two women, and then praises himself for that action
- The leader who realizes there are no BIPOC members of a committee and so stops to find one, even though they work in a different department and have no experience in the work of the committee

This is by no means an inclusive list of all microaggressions or of identities impacted by microaggressions. The list of experiences and examples is too long for just one chapter, or even an entire book. However, regardless of the example, we can be assured that both microaggression and its resultant harm originated in a Filter.

Reflection and Action

To provide strategies for the receiver, we look to the field of trauma and tactics or strategies that help us move back to our parasympathetic nervous system. Some of these may seem trivial, but each recommendation has research supporting its positive effects.

- **Deep breathing:** Practice full and slow diaphragmatic breathing, with a deep inhale through the mouth, holding for a few seconds, and a long exhale through the nose.
- **Meditation:** Practice mindfulness, guided meditation, or self-meditation.

- **Nature:** Be outside amidst nature, take in the sounds of birds, or even walk barefoot on the ground.
- **Physical activity:** Get up and moving to kick in the cardiovascular system.
- **Psychotherapy:** Seek professionals who are trained in trauma care.

For the sender, the strategies to address the source of the microaggression depend on the type of Filter harm it creates.

Filter Associations

- Intentionally, consciously create counter-stereotypical associations.
- Process afterward. What Filters were at play? How and where did you get caught in a Filter association?

Lack of Associations

- Be curious and question:
  - Know your patterns of bias, and question them in your beliefs and behaviors. Be self-critical.
  - Be curious of patterns. The deeper the complexity, the less judgment we tend to have. There's even more benefit when you look for deeper complexity in Filters; for example, X group tends to express leadership in this way, Y group expresses in that way. If we can see that neither is inherently good or bad, then we can allow for both/and—good leaders can come from both X group and Y group.

Lack of Exposure

- Expose yourself to differences. But remember—exposure doesn't equal competence, so it's not just exposure to Frames but also understanding of Filters.

- ○ That exposure can be through interactions but also through movies or books.
- ○ Warning: be careful not to be a cultural tourist or voyeur. Start with the assumption that you are the different one.
- ○ Just as not every person you meet in a new city is not (or has no desire to be) a tour guide and may even be very tired of tourists, not every person from a cultural group wants to educate you, and few may have the skills of being a guide. It's not the guide's responsibility or the city's responsibility for you to understand it; it's your responsibility, so do your homework, and don't waste their time having them tell you things you can easily find out from other resources.
- Be open to what's new.
- ○ Look for new patterns and new associations.
- ○ Ask yourself, "Can I consider the possibility that . . . ?"

Partial Consciousness

- Recognize partial consciousness: resist the urge to act or respond differently until you have practiced in low-risk situations.

CHAPTER 9

FILTER-DRIVEN ORGANIZATIONS

Most of us as individuals are unknowingly controlled by our Filters, stalled in the third stage of development with a focus on similarities. Clueless to that lack of ability yet with the best of intentions, we come together in organizations and communities to create, work, and solve problems.

That Filter-driven, oblivious lack of development doesn't get left at the door as we enter. It follows us into the organizations we're part of, seeping into our interactions as well as the work and structures we create. The result is organizational structures that reflect that same lack of development and that same obliviousness to Filters, creating ineffectiveness and inequity that is further amplified when our organizations combine into systems.

Filter-driven individuals create Filter-driven organizations. And the same Filter tools that work for individuals can be used and modified for organizations to create greater equity.

Let's go back to the classroom of kids working to solve a sixth-grade problem. We already have the vocal second graders who are causing a distraction; now let's add a few more dynamics that also reflect our real-life situation in organizations. First, almost all the rest of the students are third graders, including the class leaders. But there's no teacher in the room to guide and no answer sheet at the end for them to check their work.

If they don't have the ability to solve the sixth-grade problem, they will rarely, if ever, get the right answer. Yet with no teacher and no answer sheet, they'll never know *that* their answers are wrong, *how* they are wrong, or *how to get to* the right answer.

Does it matter that they really *want* to get the answer right? No. Because the skill isn't there to match the will.

When they have new problems that build on previous problems, the wrong answers are amplified, all unknowingly. Over time, they'll end up creating an echo chamber that convinces everyone that the wrong answer is the right answer. They may even collaborate with other third-grade classrooms, all justifying their wrong answers and continuing the amplification and implications of those wrong answers.

Would someone please just teach them the necessary math!

Organizational Frames and Filters

The concept of Frames and Filters carries over to organizations as well (see figure 9.1). Frames are easy to observe and are what we are conscious of. At an organization's group level, those are the patterns of demographic differences that we can easily identify. As an example, substantially more of X group are in leadership, while substantially more of Y group are in entry-level positions.

Those are easy-to-observe differences that we are often conscious of on a group level.

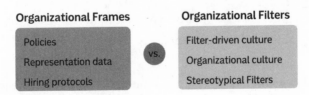

Organizational Frames

Policies

Representation data

Hiring protocols

vs.

Organizational Filters

Filter-driven culture

Organizational culture

Stereotypical Filters

Figure 9.1 Organizational Frames and Filters

Another Frame in organizations is written policies and practices. Those are easily visible and also result from the Filters that created them.

Filters, on the other hand, include the organizational culture that drives the behavior in the organization. As an example, one of our clients works in an industry that requires them to have a very risk-averse, rules-driven culture, while another client has a very risk-taking, rules-bending culture. In the former, they'll require five to six meetings with us prior to a presentation to review and refine the content, and our partners in the organization may even want us to do a dry run with them to know every word we're going to say. In the latter, we can show up and do our thing without any pre-meetings or extensive reviews.

While the organizational culture can play a significant role in an organization's ability to create equity, that's not where I want to focus.

Organizational cultures vary widely, but regardless of the culture and organization, what is consistently pervasive across organizations is a foundational culture reflective of the third stage of development—a Filter-driven culture where Systemic Filters can seep in and influence decisions and interactions.

Filter-Driven Culture

When individuals oblivious to their Filters come together in an organization, the weaknesses of their Filter-driven behavior carry over and are amplified on a broader level, creating a Filter-driven culture.

The markers of a Filter-driven organization stem from the lack of ability of the individuals within it.

- Filters continue to create decisions, but now they are organizational decisions.

- The high-will/low-skill dynamic is reflected organizationally as well. The organization may want, or at least say they want, to be diverse and inclusive, yet they never actually achieve that and instead continue to spin their wheels in tractionless transactions.
- They assume similarity and one-size-fits-all approaches, particularly with policies and practices, and are unable to differentiate or allow for differentiation.
- They are unable to recognize biased policies and practices, and even less able to change them to be more equitable.
- They take an equality-based approach (see chapter 11).
- A misplaced focus on the positive intent of the organization creates an environment ripe for microaggressions to flourish.

Square Peg, Round Hole

While Miguel and I were excited to buy it for our first baby because it was a learning toy, I don't think any of our kids played with it too much. Meant to teach them shapes and hand-eye coordination, it was a hollow red sphere with multiple holes of different shapes. The corresponding yellow blocks or pegs fit those holes—circles, squares, stars, and triangles. Once the kids got to a certain age, the toy would get tossed aside because it became boring. They knew, of course, that a square block couldn't fit into the round hole. It was obvious.

If only the same games in our organizations were so obvious.

Organization after organization has created a culture of, for, and by only round holes, yet they say they want square and triangle and star pegs. When the peg isn't allowed to enter or doesn't want to stay, the organization blames it on the peg: "They just weren't a good fit," or "Well, we tried to hire some of *them*, and *they* just wouldn't stay."

Just as Filter-driven individuals are oblivious to the rigidity that comes with their inability to adapt, Filter-driven organizations are oblivious to the rigidity that comes with their Filter-driven culture.

Filter-driven cultures developed only to the third stage tend to hire for diversity yet onboard and promote for conformity. That red spherical toy then adds another dimension of a second sphere, one inside the other. The outer sphere has all different kinds of holes—squares, circles, triangles, and stars—so it more easily allows differences in Frame—gender, race, religion, color, sexual orientation, and so on—to enter. But then the inner sphere of the Filter-driven culture is made up of only circle holes.

The culture can't actually take in the full resources that come with all the different pegs. In fact, it blocks them from full inclusion. What results are patterns we see across organizations that are telltale signs of a Filter-driven culture.

- What we consistently hear in focus groups is people from non-dominant groups expressing that they have to work harder, giving more than 100 percent yet perceived as performing at much less, continually being passed over for promotion while people from dominant groups with less experience are advanced.
- Microaggressions are commonly experienced by people from nondominant groups.[1]
- On aggregate, individuals believe they are inclusive and respectful of differences yet also on aggregate believe their colleagues who are different aren't fully included.
- There is a focus on fairness versus differentiated approaches, and on inputs versus outcomes (see chapter 11).
- There is a lack of diversity in leadership.
- The majority of individuals are unaware of identity-based experience, thus the experiences of marginalization are minimized or disregarded.

What You Say Isn't Always What Is Heard

Let's look at just communication as an example. There are four cultural styles of communication and conflict. As cultural styles, these are Group Filters. Basically, direct or indirect preference is combined with either an emotionally expressive or emotionally restrained preference.[2] As a Group Filter, the groups we belong to teach us one style or another, grooming us through social norms that establish expectations for our behavior Those norms and expectations are stored in our Filters, determining the communication style we believe is *right*, *good*, or *professional*.

When we interact with someone exhibiting the behaviors of the opposite communication preference, our Filters then tell us that behavior is *wrong, bad*, or *unprofessional*. Those negative Filter evaluations of their behavior can then expand into negative Filter evaluations about the person as a whole, sometimes even to the entire identity group of that person.

And if we have developed only to the third stage, those Filter judgments are left unchallenged.

What happens, then, if most individuals in an organization have developed only to the third stage and prefer the same communication style? That style becomes policy. Those filters are then validated and reinforced through the structures of the organization. They become the *right* way, the *professional* way, the *respectful* way to communicate.

In the United States, the predominant style perceived as respectful is direct and emotionally restrained. In conflict, that means going straight to the person and telling them face-to-face, with no significant change in tone, volume, or expression, explicitly what the issue is. The person might say they are very angry, but their body language and tone might look and sound the same as it would if they were saying they were ecstatic.

That's an example of communication in conflict. In regular communication, an emotionally restrained person will wait several milliseconds after the person they are conversing with ends a thought before responding. This signals that they are listening and engaged. The person who is expressive, however, will talk at the same time as the other individual to signal they are listening and engaged in what the other is saying. It's similar to the call-and-response or the "Amen! Preach it!" as the preacher is preaching.

Over and over again, we see US-based organizations with *effective communication* or *productive conflict* policies that essentially are lists of the behaviors of this dominant US style, even in global, international, or multinational US-based organizations.

That's a round-hole policy, and it's just one example.

But let's go deeper into that example because the Filter fit also translates to Frames. White people in the United States tend to prefer the direct and emotionally restrained style, while African Americans tend to prefer the direct and emotionally expressive style.[3] That expressiveness means emotions are externalized through bigger, more expressive body language as well as noticeable changes in tone, volume, and tenor of speech.

Opposite behaviors, yet the same level of emotion and positive intent.

Let's put a few points together now, in the situation of a classroom. A Black, emotionally expressive student is excited about the content being taught, feeling engaged with the teacher and so interjects as the teacher is speaking. They also externalize their frustration when homework they don't like is doled out, unlike their White counterparts, who, while just as frustrated, don't express it outwardly. That student, like most Black students, has a White teacher[4] who is likely emotionally restrained. If that teacher is like the majority, they are only developed to the third stage and oblivious to the Filters involved in any given interaction.

To the emotionally restrained Filters of the teacher who has yet to develop, that interjection is rude and disrespectful, so they feel stressed every time it happens, thinking their authority in the classroom is being challenged. Combine that with the likelihood that they unknowingly hold the stereotypical Filter that associates Black with harm, and it's easy to see why more Black students are removed from the classroom and even from school through expulsion.[5]

We'll come back to this example when we look at equity, but in the meantime, let's note all the factors that were involved:

- **Difference of Frame:** White and Black
- **Difference of Filter:** emotionally restrained and emotionally expressive
- **Systemic Filter:** associating Black with harm
- **Third-stage ability:** inability to see and respond to the Filters that are creating the situation

When _This_ Doesn't Lead to _That_ in Organizations, or Organizationally Sanctioned Filters

Organizationally, supervisors and managers will focus on a particular behavior, missing the Filters that created them. _Stop doing this. Start doing that._ When the _this_ continues and the _that_ doesn't emerge, most people tend to blame the person and, as I did with my mother-in-law, attach the Filter judgment holistically to the person.

More broadly in organizations, we create policies and handbooks that dictate behaviors without regard for the varying Filters. In doing so, we sanction just one type of Filter, likely the Filter common to the dominant group.

We can see the absurdity in that with individual Filters. Imagine an organization that had policies stating no one could make any small talk at the beginning of a meeting regardless of who's meeting or why. Naomi would love it, and Ted would struggle. There might even be flags in Ted's performance reviews about his inability to follow the policy.

Sounds ludicrous, right?

Yet we frequently see *unstated yet still firmly rooted practices* that sanction only certain Filters:

- Continually favoring one very specific type of experience
- Restricting remote work even when not necessary
- Hiring from the same university
- Deeming only one career path as valid: *this* degree or *that* certification

We also see Group Filters make their way into policies all the time. As an example, the behaviors of direct communication are frequently sanctioned through communications policies in countless organizations.

Square peg. Round hole.

When the Emperor Has No Clothes

We predicted it would happen and we explicitly warned them, but there was nothing they could do about it.

As a large nonprofit organization serving a very diverse clientele, DEI was very important to them. Our work was to take key divisions through our developmental process to build their cultural competence and their ability to more clearly see and respond to Filters, thus setting them up for more effective interactions within their workplace and with their clients and enabling them to create more equitable processes.

It was their director of organizational development who brought us in and set us up with the first groups. While our process was highly successful, the more groups we worked with and the more groups we developed, the more that became a problem.

That's because those groups were at lower levels in the organization and didn't include top leadership. The mistaken belief of those leaders was that, as successful leaders, they didn't need to develop. Just staff, particularly staff working most closely with clients, needed to develop.

Yet by developing only the lower levels, we were creating a top-heavy developmental drag on the organization. As those lower in the organization advanced, leaders were getting left behind developmentally.

The amazing thing about our Filters is that they are ubiquitous, yet they are also unrevealed to those who have yet to develop. So, once we develop and experience them all around us, everywhere all the time, we can become baffled that others remain clueless. In addition, as our society perpetuates and reinforces ineffective Filter-driven behavior and stage-three sound bites, once we have developed, those messages and behaviors that were always there before suddenly become glaring in their ineffectiveness.

What we predicted came true. Folks lower in the organization who had developed could now hear that ineffective speak coming from their leaders; they could see how their leaders were clueless to their own Filters dictating their behavior.

Suddenly, the emperor had no clothes.

As with individuals, organizations need to develop to be more effective, make better decisions, and create equity. Because the developmental bar in organizations is set by its leaders, if they have only developed to the third stage, the organization will be stuck there too.

They might do lots of work, set up activities, and create a strategy, but all that work will gain them no traction.

So, where do we start organizational work? With leaders.

Not only do they set the bar, but leaders also have the positional power to institute change, adjust policies and practices, and set a new tone in the organization.

After developing the leaders, the next step for organizations is to develop the individuals within them. Typically, when starting our work, we measure the level of development of at least a representative sample of the organization, and we see a bell curve. The apex of most individuals is typically in the third stage. We move that apex of the organization by moving the individuals within it.

Filter-Driven Systems

Filter-driven individuals come together and create Filter-driven organizations that, in turn, combine to create Filter-driven systems.

What we can easily observe are the disparities and patterns of advantage and disadvantage. Across systems, inequities and disparities are rampant. Easy to observe means those patterns and the evidence are the Frames. Once again, the driver of those Frames are Filters.

How do we address these extreme inequities that have progressively widened in so many aspects of our lives? It's easy to become immobilized by the enormity of inequities, or even give in to helplessness and apathy, believing there is nothing we as individuals can do.

But there *is* something we can *all* do.

We start by understanding how systemic inequities are created and then, most importantly, understand and accept accountability for the through line between our own Filters and those inequities.

Let's start by defining two pairs of terms that are often conflated, confused, or used interchangeably. To better understand that through line, it's important to distinguish between these concepts.

We'll start with *bias* versus *inequities*. **Bias is an input while inequities are an outcome.** I imagine bias as a seed that, with the assistance of key elements, creates the weeds we don't want, which are the inequities.

Bias gives favor or advantage to one group over another or one individual over another based on their identity. Because bias seeps into our thoughts and actions through our Filters, it's helpful to remember the different types of Filters. If I hire someone because they wear purple polka dots to an interview and my Individual Filters then create a positive association for them, that one Filter-driven decision, while still illogical, is just one drop in an ocean and doesn't add to the ripple effect that a Systemic Filter would because there isn't a broader pattern of advantage for people who wear purple polka dots—or, for that matter, of disadvantage for those who don't.

It's when our bias is fueled by our Systemic Filters that we contribute to the wave of inequities if we are unable to check and challenge those Filters.

Inequities are evidence of the patterns of bias driven by Systemic Filters. They show a lack of parity in results or outcomes observable on a larger scale, after the fact.

Two other terms that are often conflated or used interchangeably are *systems* and *structures*. Once again, distinguishing between the two helps us see the through line created by our Filters. **Individuals create structures; multiple structures then combine to make up systems.**

Structures are groups and organizations together with their scaffolding of policies, practices, norms, and hierarchies. When those policies, as they often do, reinforce stereotypical bias, they contribute to the patterns of inequities we see on a systemic level.

The educational system, as an example, is a complex web of structures such as individual schools, companies that support schools, school boards, universities, testing organizations, and the list goes on. Each of these structures is made up of individuals: students, teachers, staff, administrators, policymakers, faculty, and again, the list goes on.

If one leader, regardless of gender, holds the stereotypical Filter that associates women with family and home and if that leader has not developed the ability to recognize, challenge, and shift that Filter, they are more likely to make a biased decision to promote a male candidate over an equally or even more qualified female candidate. That one biased decision contributes to the inequity of a lack of women in leadership in that particular organization, which in turn contributes to the inequity of a lack of women in leadership on a larger scale of the system of the overall workforce.

Until 2023, women made up less than 10 percent of Fortune 500 CEOs.[6] That inequitable outcome was fueled by the seed of countless biased individual decisions and biased structures of policies, practices, and norms. Put the concepts together: bias in our structures, created by our Systemic Filters, leads to structural inequities as well as to bias in our systems, which in turn leads to systemic inequities.

When centuries of intentional—even, at times, legal—discrimination is a significant driver of these inequities, what can any of us do about it?

We can start by challenging our own Filters.

Reflection and Action

Try to identify the organizationally sanctioned Filters in your workplace. Over the next several days, pay attention to the unwritten rules that drive behaviors or the patterns of preference throughout the organization. Is there a link between those patterns and broader inequities in the organization?

GREATER INDIVIDUAL EFFECTIVENESS

He said it was like seeing the side-by-side before-and-after images of himself after an extreme makeover. The difference was shocking. Yet for Thomas, his wasn't a makeover involving stylists with a new hairdo and makeup. His was the difference in how he perceived and responded to a difference with the ability to Filter Shift.

Thomas was a high-level director at one of the organizations we were working with. He had completed our Filter Shift development process along with other leaders in the organization and had developed from the third to the sixth stage. I happened to see him in the hallway months later. He hurried over as soon as he saw me to relay his story.

It was a story about Abbas, a colleague who had recently joined his team and had just immigrated from Iraq. Thomas wanted to ensure he felt welcome, so he and his wife invited Abbas to their home for dinner.

The evening proceeded well, and Thomas appreciated the opportunity to get to know his new colleague. So, as he closed the door behind him at the end of Abbas' visit, he was feeling good, appreciating the evening and the connection with his colleague.

That's when the image of stark before-and-after contrast showed up. But it wasn't Thomas in the before image; it was his wife and her reaction. As soon as he closed the door, he heard an exclamation from the kitchen. His wife had started cleaning up from their dinner and exhaled a loud, "Thank God! I thought he was never going to leave!"

He was confused.

From his perspective, it had been a wonderful evening. Yet it was obvious his wife was not only relieved it was over but also appeared very agitated. He didn't even need to ask because before he had reached the kitchen, she had already started to reveal what he would later call the "before image." It was an image of how he too would have reacted just months prior, before learning to Filter Shift.

"I can't believe how rude he was! I mean, I was fine with the pleasantries at the beginning of the meal, but then, that whole thing about the war. After that, I honestly checked out of the rest of the conversation.

"I mean, you asked him about how he and other Iraqis tend to perceive the wars with the United States, and he didn't even answer you! He just got all hot and bothered, yelling as he told some kinda story about a lion and sheep! Seriously!? I hate to say it, but I can see why they have so many problems over there!"

Thomas then went on to tell me his perspective of the story. "Abbas just had a different cultural style of communication, and I could see it clearly. Even before I asked him about the wars, and before his response of a story, I had noted that he was emotionally expressive and that he was an indirect communicator.

"When I asked him about the United States and our interventions and wars in his country, Abbas showed me through his expressiveness that he really cared about the topic. I didn't see it as yelling; I saw it as passion about the topic. And the story? Well, clearly the

United States was the lion, and the Iraqis were the sheep. In the story, he kept saying how lions and sheep have complex relationships. At times, the lion is needed to protect the sheep, yet at other times, the lion also unknowingly turns on the sheep.

"He didn't want to be disrespectful of the United States to state it so explicitly, so he told the story to be more respectful. What I understood is that he's passionate about the topic and that he appreciates the US involvement but that there are times he believes we've overstepped or made things worse.

"Had this same interaction happened several months before I understood Filters, I would have reacted to Abbas the same way my wife did. I was amazed, and it really is true! It's not about me giving up my values but about adding new ways to see and respond. And yes, I'm sure I will be less likely to discriminate or stereotype, which will help those who are marginalized in our organization, but very selfishly, I know *my* experience that night was so much more positive for *me*."

How to Filter Shift

How do you develop to that stage where you can adapt as Thomas did?

As I was "growing up" in the cultural competence field, I was always told that the best practice was to spend 40 hours of intentional development work to develop at least one stage. That development work would include learning about a multitude of different groups. One day you might learn about introverts versus extroverts. Another day you might learn about different cultures by race or by country or generations. Do that for 40 hours, best practice would suggest, and you will likely develop.

Because that was best practice, that's what we did for a number of years with hundreds of participants. Thankfully, those participants developed. But what started to become clear for me was that everyone seemed to wrestle with the same key concepts, and once people were able to get past those, the "aha" moments started to spark and they were able to develop.

So, we redesigned our development process to focus on those key concepts, and when we did, we reduced the time necessary for development from 40 hours down to just 9.

I detailed those in *Filter Shift*.[1] I've also woven them throughout this book. They all roll up into the Filter Shift process. You've read about each of these in depth with examples, but let's look at them all together at a high level.

1. SEE Self: Acknowledge and Accept Accountability for Our Filters

This first step is the biggest and most difficult because we are starting to use our brain differently. Most of us aren't even aware of our Filters, so just learning that they exist and how they are designed to function is a significant insight for many. Normalizing that function allows us to acknowledge our own Filters without feeling blame or shame.

Knowing Filters exist is one thing, but the real impact comes as we begin to witness our own Filters in action. The Active Conscious process and the SEE model allow us to do that and to stop the automatic process directed by our Filters so that we can challenge them. Whether we examine our thoughts in the moment or after the fact by listing our expectations and descriptions, the process of separating objective from subjective thoughts is still the same:

1. **Stop to be conscious of our thoughts**, even listing them out after the fact.
2. **Separate the thoughts that are subjective.** Those are the thoughts that Explain and Evaluate, which is the telltale sign that they are coming from our Filters.

3. **Challenge the subjective thoughts coming from our Filters** by focusing on what we are left with, the objective See or observe. Those are the thoughts that everyone, regardless of their Filters, would agree to. Almost always, those are few to none of the items on the list.

One other key concept we need to be aware of in order to fully understand our Filters is how they are shaped by our own past experiences. Because we don't all have the same past experiences, our Filters can never perceive the situations we're in now in the same way. That means we have identity-based experiences. If we want to be a full partner in creating equity, regardless of our identity, that reality can't be ignored.

This leads to the last key concept of SEE Self, which is to accept accountability. My Filters are mine; only mine. And they direct my behaviors. If I want those behaviors to be the most effective and equitable, I'm the only one who can shift my Filters to create that change.

2. SEE Others: Assume Difference without Judgment

Our Filters unconsciously assume similarity. To counterbalance that automatic process, we must consciously assume difference and look for greater complexity.

1. I am different, not the norm.
2. My Filters may be wrong, so I assume different from what my Filters tell me. I challenge my Filters.
3. The other person has Filters different from mine, and their behaviors are relative to them and their Filters, not mine.

We also need to move away from the judgmental evaluations our Filters make. The best way to do that is to both assume positive intent coming from others as well as to question the impact of our own Filter-driven behaviors.

3. Shift Actions: Shift Behavior to Be More Effective

What frequently keeps us from actually approaching situations differently is our concern that the differentiation wouldn't be fair or that it is stereotypical. The more we become adept at challenging our Filters, the easier that differentiation will be.

But then, we need to actually shift our behavior, which, frankly, takes practice. We first need to ensure we are ready to shift our actions and behaviors. We do so by asking three key questions:

1. Am I **capable**?
   Can I see the difference in Filters without judgment and fully accept that my approach is not the norm, but just one option?
2. Am I **comfortable**?
   Do I feel comfortable responding differently? If not, my actions may be perceived as insincere.
3. Have I considered the **consequences**?
   If the consequences are too high, then this isn't the time for me to step out of my known approach.

We need to answer yes to each of these questions before we actually shift our behavior. In the case of Thomas, he said he was able to answer yes to all the questions when it came to shifting to indirect communication with Abbas. So he did by responding to Abbas within the metaphor of the lion and sheep. But when it came to being more emotionally expressive, he just wasn't comfortable yet.

So, he chose to compromise.

If we are not able to fully answer yes to all three questions, then we must follow the three steps to compromise:

1. **Continue**: I continue using the same behavior I would normally use.
2. **Cite** difference: I acknowledge the different approaches, mine and that of the other, both as equally valid.
3. **Clarify** shared intent and goal: I state the shared goal and/or shared positive intent.

For Thomas, that meant he continued to be emotionally restrained but was able to let Abbas know that the restraint was his natural way of communicating and that the topic of the wars was important to him as well, but that he just expressed that concern differently.

How to Be an Ally

One of the topics both individuals of all identities as well as organizations of all industries frequently ask us about is how to be an ally. I'll admit, it's a request that frequently makes me cringe, particularly when it's asked by folks who haven't done any development work. You tell me.

Can I be an ally to you if I don't understand the impact I have on you?

No.

Can I be an ally to you if I don't understand that you have a different identity-based experience than me?

No.

Can I be an ally to you if I don't understand your Filters and how to respond differently to them?

No.

I know the topic of allyship is popular. I also know there is a positive intent in asking for the work. Yet the request is akin to a second grader asking for sixth-grade homework. I don't want to discourage them, but they just aren't ready for it.

I also believe that if we want to be allies, the first thing we need to do is make sure we aren't committing microaggressions ourselves. So, let's go back to the four types of Filter harm that cause microaggressions, and I'm going to give some quick strategies for how to address each.

Filter associations: Because we may consciously disagree with a stereotype, we most likely won't know if or when we have a specific stereotypical association. What we can do is consciously, actively challenge it with an opposing association. We can also actively counter it when we see it represented in the media. Reject the stereotype, and replace it with the positive association consciously.

Lack of associations: Watch for the telltale sign of a lack of association, which is surprise. Challenge yourself to consider the possibility of the new association. And if someone tells you their reality, even if it's different from yours, believe it, don't challenge it or them.

Lack of exposure: Learn, build your awareness, and get more information. Reading both fiction and nonfiction about different groups or watching movies that represent different groups helps you gain awareness, and it's easy to do. So try to avoid putting the responsibility on others by asking them to teach you about their difference. Also, pay attention to the Stupid Question Syndrome. If you fall into it, recognize the lack of breadth in your understanding.

Partial consciousness: This is really about lacking the ability to respond effectively. So, ensure you don't try to change your approach if you can't answer in the affirmative all of the three questions (capable, comfortable, consequences). When you can't, then use the three steps for compromise (continue, cite, clarify), and you'll be much less likely to offend.

Reflection and Action

Start practicing the compromise steps in situations where you recognize different Filters are at play. After practicing those steps several times in different settings, you'll likely be ready to practice shifting your behavior. Even though you may be ready to shift your approach, start practicing in situations with very low consequences, like with the cashier at the store or with family members (after you forewarn them!).

CHAPTER 11

CREATING ORGANIZATIONAL EQUITY

Imagine an assembly-line engineer is asked to fix the machine that continually spits out faulty widgets. They keep reviewing the pieces going into the machine and spend their time making sure those are the right pieces and that they're going into the machine in the right order.

But the machine continues to churn faulty widgets. So, the engineer returns and once again spends their time reviewing what's going into the machine. Just to be sure it's fixed this time, they get new pieces to input into the machine. But the machine continues with its faulty production.

What are they missing?

It seems obvious, right? They haven't actually looked at what happens to those pieces once they enter the machine. They haven't fixed the real problem because all they're focused on are the inputs into the machine and not the faulty machine itself.

Why is this misstep so obvious when the actor is an engineer unable to fix a machine, yet when essentially this same misstep occurs in the systems of our organizations, so many of us miss the obvious source of the problem?

The systems within our organizations continue to churn out disparities and inequities, and all too often, those charged with fixing the problem look to the wrong source. We already know that our organizations and systems produce inequities. Evidence of those inequities is obvious across industry, sector, and size.

What's more difficult to see and even more difficult to create is equity, particularly when so many individuals and organizations misunderstand it and lack the tools to create it.

What Is Equity?

Let's start with what equity is. Equity is a measure of parity in outcomes on the large scale of structures and systems. Essentially, equity is equal outcomes, but because of existing disparities combined with the individual and structural biases built into our systems, we can't use an equality-based approach to get to that parity of outcomes.

Particularly since George Floyd's murder, more and more organizations have expressed a commitment to equity, yet so few, if any, have made significant progress.

Why?

There are many common misunderstandings about equity as well as many common missteps that keep organizations spinning their wheels in tractionless transactions, never truly transforming their organizations to be more equitable.

The Misunderstandings

Input versus Outcomes

First, like the engineer in our example, most organizations focus on the inputs. Specifically, they focus on *equality of inputs* versus *equity in outcomes*. We see this over and over again, particularly in equity of representation in an organization. I want to illustrate this problem with a graphic of inequity in organizations (see figure 11.1).

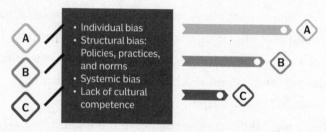

Figure 11.1   The System of Organizational Inequity

Let's say the box in the center represents an organization. We'll call it Acme Company. The A, B, and C represent different identities and intersected identities present in the organization.

Acme sincerely wants to be more equitable in representing these different identities in general and especially within their leadership ranks, so they focus on the inputs. What is the input for an organization's representation? Its hiring.

So, Acme says, let's make sure we're an equal opportunity employer and that we provide equal access to our jobs. Let's even go a step further to make sure that we recruit to create hiring slates with equal representation. That's what we see represented on the left of the box, the inputs and the focus on equal access to different identities.

Acme continues this equal access, input focus for a year, but then, in their outcomes, they see they haven't really increased representation. Identity A continues to be more represented in leadership than identity B, which is also more represented than identity C—all a reflection of their historical makeup of leadership.

What do they do? They go back to look at those inputs and ask, *What happened so that we didn't hire or promote more diversity?*

What they are missing is what is happening in the structure of the organization—that system represented by the box in between the inputs and the outcomes where a perfect storm is brewing. It's a combination of

1. individuals who are unknowingly operating with Systemic Filters;

2. those individuals not yet being developed, so they are unable to recognize and challenge those Filters as they make hiring and promotion decisions;

3. biased policies, practices, and procedures created by those individuals; and, finally,

4. a Filter-driven culture coming from the third stage of development that supports the continuation of all of the above.

Focus on Resource Allocation

Search for images of equity online. On second thought, please don't because what you'll find are lots of the same images that fall way too short in portraying this complex concept. What you'd likely see is one iteration or another of the common meme of three folks trying to see over a fence to watch a baseball game. The first person is the tallest but still can't see over the fence, the second is a bit shorter so also can't see, and the third is in a wheelchair, thus far below the site line.

In the second frame of the meme, each person is given the same-sized stepping stool, which allows only the tallest to be able to see over the fence. Then, in the third frame of the meme, each is provided with the size of stool or ramp they need to be able to see over the fence.

This meme is used by many to describe equity. It does a good job pointing out the need for moving away from equal to differentiated approaches, which we've talked about quite a bit. But the significant downside of this meme is that it also focuses on the input of resource allocation—in this case, the step or ramp.

Likely because of this meme, many organizations use resource allocation in their definitions of equity, which in turn perpetuates the myth that DEI work is just about giving more to those who are marginalized—more money, more points when hiring, more advantage all around.

If only it were that easy.

Once again, this approach only focuses on what's going into the machine versus the faulty machine itself. This approach also misses the complexity of the work needed to fix the machine of the system. So, organizations continue to get frustrated when the resources they expend don't produce the results they expect.

An Equality-Based Approach

The meme does one thing well: it distinguishes between equality and equity and clearly shows the need for differentiated approaches.

Equality applies the same rules and advantages to all in an attempt to treat everyone fairly. While used with the best of intentions, the results are rarely equal. We are often deceived by our good intentions and misled to believe that the impact on all is equally as good. While equality focuses on inputs into our systems, equity focuses on the systems themselves and the outcomes. Equity, in other words, concentrates on results.

However, what most organizations don't realize is that they don't have the ability to move beyond an equality-based approach.

That's because they have only developed to that third stage, which is all about equality, sameness, and fairness. They don't have the necessary competence to see the built-in bias in their structures or the Filter-driven culture they swim in. So, they keep working hard with those tractionless transactions, getting frustrated and maybe even giving up.

Confusing Fairness with Equity

Nearly every organization uses the word *fair* or *fairness* in their definition of equity. It makes me cringe every time I see it because it's like an emperor who has no clothes situation. They are clearly outing their third-stage development because fair is an approach of that stage.

- "No, we couldn't allow that department to work from home more than the others. That just wouldn't be fair."
- "Employees in our administrative offices will have to wear close-toed shoes just like our employees in our clinics. It wouldn't be fair otherwise."
- "To be fair, all departments have to make a 3 percent cut in their budget across the board."

These are quotes I have heard from leadership who have yet to develop past the third stage. Fairness is the excuse the third-stage mindset uses to continue an equality-based approach.

Fairness is the opposite of differentiation, which is what is necessary for us to achieve equity.

Not Considering the Ability Needed to Solve the Problem

Just because I enjoy balancing my checkbook, does that alone make me capable of creating a new financial system for my organization?

No. Only those who have organizational financial acumen have that ability.

Just because I have lived with knee pain for decades and can clearly see the evidence that validates that pain—from the arthritis visible in X-rays and MRI images to the creaking that's louder than the floorboards as I climb the stairs—does that alone mean I'm capable of giving myself, or anyone else for that matter, a knee replacement?

No. Only those who have the ability to perform a knee replacement are capable.

It's clear that creating an organizational financial system or performing knee replacement surgery are both difficult things to do, so they require extensive knowledge, experience, and practice.

How does that relate to equity work in organizations?

Achieving equity is incredibly difficult. Honestly, I think it's much more difficult than creating an organizational financial system or performing a knee replacement. Yet all too often we see organizations that turn their equity work over to individuals or groups with far less ability than the orthopedic surgeon or the CFO, just because they are cheerleaders for equity or more directly experience the inequities.

That alone, without the ability to counter inequities, isn't enough.

Overall, what organizations and communities miss is what's creating inequity and what we can influence: the biased structures fueled by our Filters and a lack of development.

Creating Equity

We know that as individuals, we need to slow down to catch up to the speed of bias. The same is true for groups and organizations. Bias leading to inequities happens quickly. Checking our Filters to create equity takes time.

In addition to slowing down, we need to reduce the vacuum of identity-based experience and instead enlist as many perspectives as reasonably possible.

Put those two together, and in an ideal situation, we have a group that has developed to the latter stages of competence, that intentionally walks through a process to more thoroughly review decisions, policies, practices, and more.

Equity Framework

To guide those groups, I developed an Equity Framework. Its goal is to produce the most equitable outcome possible in any given scenario.

The framework is an organizational modification of the Filter Shift framework for individuals. It is designed to be used by those who have developed to the latter stages of cultural competence to evaluate any given decision, policy, or practice. The framework realistically embraces continued institutional and structural changes of policies and programming while emphasizing underrepresented groups.

To promote and implement this framework throughout any organization, it is essential to have dialogue around the understanding of equity as well as to grasp the definition of key terms. This dialogue should be driven by leadership, directors, managers, and supervisors as they become experts of the Equity Framework and as they progress developmentally in cultural competence.

What Is the Issue?

Identify the policy you are evaluating or describe in detail the current situation, decision, or practice that needs to be made, written, or changed. Who is involved? What goals or outcomes are being sought?

SEE Self

- Look at the stated policy or your descriptors, and use the SEE model (See, Explain, Evaluate) to determine what comes from your unconscious Filters. What unconscious biases do you have?
- How do you define success? Is your definition of success connected to your filters? Your identity? If so, how?
- What power do you or your group have in this situation? How might that influence your definition of success?
- How will you be impacted by the proposed solutions?

Answer individually and, if pertinent, for your group or organization.

SEE Others

Consider all the stakeholder groups involved in this issue. Ideally, all groups are included in this process. If they are not, answer these questions for each group:

- How do you think they would describe the issue? Specifically, how would their Filters attach different explanations and evaluations to the issue?
- How might they define success differently than you do?
- What power do these groups currently have in this situation? What power have they historically had?
- How will they be impacted by the proposed solutions?
- What related disparities have these groups experienced?

Shift Actions

- Are you aware of the historical context related to this issue and any decisions, policies, or structures that have been established to increase disparities?
- Consider intersecting identities and systems. For example, if your stakeholder group is Latines, consider how Latina women versus Latino men may be impacted differently. If your decision lies in one system (e.g., education), consider how other systems (e.g., economics) have impacted this stakeholder group.
- What existing policies or practices may erode equity gains from your decision, policy, or practice?
- What decision, process, or structure can you implement that will most likely ensure equity?
- Does the proposed action affect any institutional norms or systems in the organization? If so, how?

- What method or metrics can you use to track the effects of the policy or program?
- Are there potential negative organizational or social outcomes? If so, what strategies can you put in place to mitigate these negative outcomes?

Reflection and Action

Apply this Equity Framework to your own organization. Start with written policies, guidelines, or practices. Because they are already established, you can take your time practicing with them. Once you feel comfortable, move to decisions that need to be made. Those are more real-time and so require more adeptness.

CHAPTER 12

WHAT ARE YOU WAITING FOR?

So now what?

You have all the tools. Now it's up to you to apply them to be more effective as an individual and to contribute to greater equity.

I know—even with the tools, there are still certain roadblocks that I commonly see holding people back. The good news is, each one has strategies you can apply to get around them.

Don't Feel Authentic?

It's a reaction I hear frequently. *If I change my approach, then I'm not being authentic.* But let's think of this analogy:

Imagine you are asked to send the same message to three different people. One is a kid in your life. The other is a colleague, and the third is your boss's boss. Would you use the same language in each message? Would you even use the same modality to send the message?

I'm guessing not.

Likely, you'll send a text to the kid versus an email to the colleague and maybe a letter to your boss's boss. And that letter likely wouldn't include memes and emojis like the text to the child would. Yet in using different modalities and different language with each, would you feel less authentic?

I'm guessing not.

That's akin to what we do when we shift our Filters to respond differently. We meet the person where they're at with what makes sense to them. And what makes sense to them? That's decided by their Filters.

So what's the strategy here? Once again, it's practicing in low-risk situations to build your comfort level.

Lack Confidence?

When lack of will is because of a lack of confidence, remember that skill builds will. So make sure you are fully seeing your Filters and the Filters of others, and start practicing. Keep in mind that you can practice in low-risk situations, such as with the cashier or with close friends and family whom you've warned about what you're doing.

Nervous Others Will Misinterpret?

When we have positive intent, the last thing we want to do is offend someone. As most people have developed only to the third stage, most people don't want to talk about differences and can easily misinterpret any discussion of difference as judgmental, even if it's not.

The tool to use here is to signal your intent and clarify. Your intent is to talk about the complexity of differences without judgment. So, clarify that with the group before you talk. It might be a statement such as:

> We're going to be talking about how this decision will impact the workforce. Our workforce isn't homogeneous. Different identities or groups or departments are impacted differently. I want us to be able to talk about those differences without sweeping them under the rug or without judgment. Can we all agree to that?

During the conversation, you might also need to remind people if you see them getting uncomfortable: *I want us to have a space where it's okay to talk about differences when we're not judging those differences.*

Concerned about Resistance?

If you're held back because you're concerned others will be resistant, I have three tools for you.

The first is used in anticipation of the resistance, before it even happens. It's inoculation. That is, a controlled small dose of something you don't want taking over uncontrollably. In a way, it's pre-empting the resistance.

As an example, I recently gave a presentation to a group of executives, and my contact in the organization had informed me ahead of time that one of the executives didn't like the term *cultural competence* because it implies incompetence. This is common, by the way!

So, when I first used the term *cultural competence,* I said:

Some will say that calling it cultural competence *is uncomfortable because it implies incompetence, suggesting we use terms like* awareness *or* sensitivity *instead. Honestly, that's common, and it comes from a lot of the blame and shame and baggage that has been built up around any DEI topic.*

Just think about other ways we very comfortably use competence. *One of them is when we talk about leadership competencies. You don't hear people uncomfortable with that because it suggests incompetence or suggesting instead we use* leadership awareness *or* leadership sensitivity.

We are actually talking about a competence, an ability, and it's an ability any of us can develop.

You're Ready!

If you are able to see Filters at play in any given situation and you have used the aforementioned strategies to get beyond the typical roadblocks, then you're ready. You can contribute to equity with your individual actions and decisions. Remember to always start with yourself.

Start with Self

Individually

Remember the Nike syndrome. If you try to jump to *just do it* before you fully see your own Filters or the Filters of others, your actions, decisions, and behaviors will likely be inauthentic, ineffective, and maybe even offensive.

Always ground yourself first in an understanding of your Filters. Remember to challenge them before you look to others. How do *my* Filters create *my* reality, *my* thoughts, *my* decisions, and *my* actions?

Starting with self is also about accountability. It's easy to look to others, especially those with more power than us, and shake our heads at them in disgust because we don't see them doing enough.

The only behavior we can positively control is our own. Likewise, the only accountability we can expect is our own.

Some will resist this saying, but it's a two-way street. *Why do I have to change if others don't?* I've heard this often enough that I've created a standard response.

If it literally is a two-way street you're driving down and you see the obstacles that the other driver doesn't see, are you really going to refuse to drive around the obstacles just because the other driver isn't? If they think it's a one-way street and are headed right at you, are you really going to entrench yourself in the belief of *I don't have to change if they don't have to change?*

Start with self.

Organizationally

Organizationally, we also need to start with self. That is, we need to look internally to our own policies, practices, environment, and patterns of inequities.

Do we have a Filter-driven culture? How is that evident? How does it create inequities? How does that in turn contribute to broader inequities?

Is it a big task?

Yup!

Is it difficult?

Yup!

As difficult as it is, organizations need to start with accountability, just as individuals do. What do you want to contribute to in your community, your systems, our world? Do you want to contribute to greater inequity or greater equity?

Inequities in our world are rampant, and it's easy to be overwhelmed, easy to sit back thinking you can't make a difference.

If not you, then who?

If we're all waiting around for someone else to start, then no one is starting. If we're all waiting for someone else to do something, then no one is doing something. If we're all waiting for someone else to address inequities, then no one is.

Be the someone else who starts, the someone else who does something, the someone else who addresses inequities, one situation, one decision, one action at a time.

DISCUSSION GUIDE

CHAPTER 1

1. What was your initial reaction to the reality that our Filters create our thoughts, which in turn create our actions? Was it surprising? Unsettling? Or something you already were aware of?

2. One of the statements in chapter 1 was, *The vital question we each need to ask ourselves is not if but when and where I am contributing to disparities in my profession, in my system, in my community?* How would you respond to that question?

3. In chapter 1, the research cited shows that most of us are controlled by our unconscious Filters. Does that surprise you? Knowing that it's true, why do you think that is?

4. The research also shows that most of us think we are more effective than we actually are. What challenges do you think that mindset presents when we come together in groups, whether in our community or organizations?

5. Think about times when you felt others were misperceiving you or misunderstanding your intent. What did you think and feel at the time, and how did it impact you in your work?

6. How often do you think misperceptions and misunderstandings happen in your work environment? How much do they get in the way?

CHAPTER 2

1. Thinking of the Individual Filter of small talk, what is your Filter preference? Do you think small talk wastes time or enriches the work?

How strong is that Filter preference for you? Can you think of times it's gotten in the way and created frustration for you?

2. Within teams or work groups, take the time to talk about this difference and individually identify your preference. You may even want to break into groups by your preference and detail how your Filters *Explain* your preference. That is, what does it mean to you to either use the small talk or avoid it? Share those explanations with those on your team who have the opposite preference. Then *Evaluate* your preference, but this time from the perspective of others who have the opposite preference. How do you think they might perceive your behavior related to small talk?

3. What are your thoughts, feelings, and reactions about the three functions of Filters? Do they make sense? Is it difficult to imagine or believe how much your unconscious controls your thoughts and behaviors?

4. What are your thoughts about and reactions to the three types of Filters and particularly their order of progression?

5. Take the time to identify your own Frames and Filters. Remember, Frames are those things that are easily observed and that others are conscious of: our color, race, size, age, gender, and so on. Filters are what unconsciously drive your preferences and behaviors, so think about your default mode or your automatic preferences for how to show up. Think about both your Individual and Group Filters.

   a. What are the top five? Those would be the Filters that are the strongest for you or the ones that most drive your behavior.

   b. Identify your biggest opposite challenges. That is, what Filters that are different from yours challenge you most?

CHAPTER 3

1. Think about the example from Tamim Ansary about the candy he would split to give half to his sister. That's his Filter of a group orientation versus an individual orientation. Where is your own Filter preference in relationship to Group versus Individual? How does that shape your thoughts and behaviors? Does this difference show up in your workplace? If so, how?

2. Go back to the Filters you identified. Now, knowing the three types of Filters, can you identify more? And can you distinguish between Individual versus Group Filters?

3. Do you have preferences in your organization that are used to justify hiring decisions similar to those mentioned as examples?

4. Think of any individual preference assessments or personality assessments you've taken, such as:

   - Myers-Briggs Type Indicator (MBTI)
   - Insights
   - CliftonStrengths (StrengthsFinder)
   - Enneagram
   - DiSC

   How do these aspects of your personality shape your preferences for yourself or your perspective of others?

5. Can you recognize some of the country- and generation-specific examples of Filter patterns?

6. What Filters do you think you have based on your generation or your principal country of identity?

7. What Group Filters are reinforced in your organization? Do they all positively help shape the culture and environment? Are any of them biased to one or more identity groups, thus creating challenges for individuals who are not part of those groups?

8. What were your initial reactions to the Harvard IAT statistic that 75 percent of individuals associate women with home and family and men with the workplace and career? How do you think that impacts broader societal gender inequities?

CHAPTER 4

1. We all experience differences every day. What does it mean to you to know that how you experience them is typically based largely on your stage of development?

2. What were your thoughts about and reactions to the math analogies related to development? Were you surprised by any of them?

3. Review the stages of development. Which stage do you think you've developed to? Remember, nearly 70 percent of people have developed to the third stage, and almost everyone overestimates their stage of development.

4. Is the distinction between intent versus impact a new learning for you? If so, what are your reactions to that concept, both in how you think about your actions and how you interpret the actions of others?

5. Do you have an example of a Filter fight you've gotten caught in, similar to the spaghetti example?

CHAPTER 5

1. Can you think of some examples of this second, judgmental stage? Think about it in all realms of society: politics, communities, and individual relationships.

2. What specific polarization is allowed or even encouraged in your organization? It might be broad-brushstroke judgments about specific roles or departments, or it may be judgmental statements made about generations or tenure in the organization.

3. Describe situations you have experienced when fear increased polarization.

4. Have you experienced situations of the Performative Polarization? What happened, and how did it impact the group dynamics?

CHAPTER 6

1. Think of examples when you've seen someone respond to polarization with commonality. How did it shift the situation?

2. Think of ways you can use the starter statements in your own organization to diffuse situations where polarization is allowed or encouraged.

3. What are your thoughts and reactions to the data that organizations, groups, or communities are held back by the stage of development of their leaders?

4. Can you think of examples of leaders who fuel polarization? What was the result?

CHAPTER 7

1. Have you ever been in a situation like I was with John? What did you think and feel at the time, and how did you react or respond?
2. What was your reaction to the Platinum Rule versus the Golden Rule?
3. What examples can you think of that come from this stage of development? Have you heard leaders speak from this stage?
4. Taking accountability for our Filters is key to cutting the puppet strings. Yet it can be difficult for many to do. Why do you think that is?
5. Think of situations when you are part of the dominant group. It may be because of your age, education, religion, race, family status, or countless other identities. Can you imagine how your experience might be very different from those in the nondominant group? What might you be oblivious to in their experience?

CHAPTER 8

1. What examples of microaggressions have you experienced or witnessed?
2. Are there patterns of microaggressions in your workplace?
3. What are your reactions to describing microaggressions as identity-based trauma?
4. Have you ever experienced stereotype threat? What was the situation?
5. Where have you seen examples of tokenizing in your organization?

CHAPTER 9

1. Do you recognize any of the markers of a Filter-driven organization? Have you seen them in your organization?
2. What are your thoughts about and reactions to the example of a Black, emotionally expressive student responding to a White, emotionally restrained teacher? Can you recognize all the factors involved?
3. Why do you think we never see an organization that has developed more than its leaders? What challenges do you think this poses for organizations?

4. What evidence of inequities or bias do you see in your organization or community?
5. What systemic inequities are you aware of?

CHAPTER 10

1. What are your reactions to the story of Thomas, his wife, and his co-worker, Abbas? How do you think you would have responded if you were in the situation?
2. It's sometimes difficult for individuals to accept accountability for their Filters. Why do you think that might be?
3. Can you describe a time when you were able to check your Filters by recognizing the thoughts they created and then challenging those thoughts? Did it help you respond more effectively?
4. Do you agree with the assumption that we can't be allies if we haven't done any development work or if we don't understand our Filters or the Filters of others? Why or why not?

CHAPTER 11

1. Where do you see examples of a focus on inputs versus outcomes in your organization or community?
2. Have you seen leaders or organizations that take an equality-based approach? What were the results?
3. What are your reactions to the statement "fairness is the opposite of differentiation, which is what is necessary for us to achieve equity"?
4. What aspects of the Equity Framework do you think might be difficult to apply?
5. What policies or decisions do you think could be evaluated with the Equity Framework in your organization?

CHAPTER 12

1. Think about those things that typically hold us back that were outlined in chapter 12:
   - Not feeling authentic

- Lacking confidence
- Being nervous others will misinterpret
- Being concerned about resistance

2. Which of these is most difficult for you? Why?
3. What concepts do you most need to practice?

NOTES

CHAPTER 1

1. Walter Gilliam, Angela Maupin, Chin Reyes, Maria Accavitti, and Frederick Shic, *Do Early Educators' Implicit Biases Regarding Sex and Race Relate to Behavior Expectations and Recommendations of Preschool Expulsions and Suspensions?* (New Haven, CT: Yale University Child Study Center, 2016), https://www.jsums.edu/scholars/files/2017/03/Preschool-Implicit -Bias-Policy-Brief_final_9_26_276766_5379.pdf.

2. Gilliam, Maupin, Reyes, Accavitti, and Shic, *Do Early Educators' Implicit Biases Regarding Sex and Race Relate to Behavior Expectations?*

3. Mitchell R. Hammer, "Additional Cross-Cultural Validity Testing of the Intercultural Development Inventory," *International Journal of Intercultural Relations* 35, no. 4 (July 2011): 474–87, https://doi.org/10.1016/j .ijintrel.2011.02.014.

4. Hammer, "Additional Cross-Cultural Validity Testing."

5. Andrew Wiley, *Validation Analysis of the Intercultural Development Inventory (IDI)* (Las Vegas, NV: ACS Ventures, 2017), https://idiinventory .zendesk.com/hc/en-us/article_attachments/19836951718163.

6. Wiley, *Validation Analysis of the Intercultural Development Inventory (IDI).*

7. M. Keith Chen and Ryne Rohla, "The Effect of Partisanship and Political Advertising on Close Family Ties," *Science* 360, no. 6392 (June 2018): 1020–24, https://doi.org/10.1126/science.aaq1433.

8. Daniel Cox, Juhem Navarro-Rivera, and Robert P. Jones, "Race, Religion, and Political Affiliation of Americans' Core Social Networks," PRRI,

August 3, 2016, https://www.prri.org/research/poll-race-religion-politics -americans-social-networks/.

9. "2021 Hate Crime Statistics," US Department of Justice, December 12, 2022, https://www.justice.gov/hatecrimes/2021-hate-crime-statistics.

10. Wiley, *Validation Analysis of the Intercultural Development Inventory (IDI).*

11. Jason A. Okonofua and Jennifer L. Eberhardt, "Two Strikes: Race and the Disciplining of Young Students," *Psychological Science* 26, no. 5 (2015): 617–24, https://doi.org/10.1177/0956797615570365.

12. National Center for Education Statistics, "Indicator 15: Retention, Suspension, and Expulsion," US Department of Education, updated February 2019, https://nces.ed.gov/programs/raceindicators/indicator_rda .asp.

13. National Center for Education Statistics, "Public High School Graduation Rates," US Department of Education, updated May 2023, https:// nces.ed.gov/programs/coe/indicator/coi/high-school-graduation -rates#2.

14. Eder Campuzano, "New Laws Seek to Make Detentions, Suspensions Rarer in Minnesota Elementary Schools," *Star Tribune*, July 3, 2023, https://www.startribune.com/new-laws-seek-to-make-detentions-sus pensions-rarer-in-minnesota-elementary-schools/600287182/.

15. Richie Zweigenhaft, "Diversity among Fortune 500 CEOs from 2000 to 2020: White Women, Hi-Tech South Asians, and Economically Privileged Multilingual Immigrants from Around the World," Who Rules America, January 2021, https://whorulesamerica.ucsc.edu/diversity /diversity_update_2020.html.

16. "The Diversity of the Top 50 Fortune 500 CEOs over Time," Qualtrics, August 4, 2023, https://www.qualtrics.com/blog/fortune-500 -ceo-diversity/.

CHAPTER 2

1. Tor Nørretranders, *The User Illusion: Cutting Consciousness Down to Size* (London: Penguin, 1999).

2. Timothy D. Wilson, *Strangers to Ourselves: Discovering the Adaptive Unconscious* (Cambridge, MA; London: Belknap, 2002).

3. George Kelly, *The Psychology of Personal Constructs* (London; New York: W. W. Norton & Company, 1955; London; New York: Routledge in association with the Centre for Personal Construct Psychology, 1991).

4. Wilson, *Strangers to Ourselves.*

5. B. Libet, C. A. Gleason, E. W. Wright, and D. K. Pearl, "Time of Conscious Intention to Act in Relation to Onset of Cerebral Activity (Readiness-Potential): The Unconscious Initiation of a Freely Voluntary Act," *Brain* 106, no. 3 (September 1983): 623–42, https://doi.org/10.1093/brain/106.3.623.

CHAPTER 3

1. "Tamim Ansary," on Tamim Ansary's website, accessed November 21, 2023, https://www.mirtamimansary.com/.

2. Tamir Ansary, live presentation, Multicultural Development Center, Twin Cities, Minnesota, circa 2001.

3. Janet M. Bennett and Milton J. Bennett, "Developing Intercultural Sensitivity: An Integrative Approach to Global and Domestic Diversity," in *Handbook of Intercultural Training*, 3rd ed. (Thousand Oaks, CA: Sage Publications, 2004), 147–65, https://doi.org/10.4135/9781452231129.n6.

4. Lindsey Pollak, *The Remix* (New York: HarperCollins, 2019).

5. Pollak, *The Remix.*

6. Terri Morrison, Wayne A. Conaway, and George A. Borden, *Kiss, Bow, or Shake Hands: How to Do Business in Sixty Countries* (Avon, MA: Adams Media Corporation, 2002).

7. Charles Hampden-Turner and Fons Trompenaars, *Building Cross-Cultural Competence: How to Create Wealth from Conflicting Values* (Chichester, West Sussex, England: John Wiley, 2000).

8. Morrison, Conaway, and Borden, *Kiss, Bow, or Shake Hands.*

9. Fons Trompenaars and Charles Hampden-Turner, *Riding the Waves of Culture* (New York: McGraw-Hill, 1998).

10. Morrison, Conaway, and Borden, *Kiss, Bow, or Shake Hands.*

11. T. E. Deal and Allen A. Kennedy, *Corporate Cultures: The Rites and Rituals of Corporate Life* (1982; repr., New York: Basic Books, 2000).

12. Project Implicit, "Preliminary Information," harvard.edu, 2011, https://implicit.harvard.edu/implicit/takeatest.html. Accessed November 21, 2023.

13. Project Implicit, "Preliminary Information."

14. Project Implicit, "Preliminary Information."

15. Project Implicit, "Preliminary Information."

16. Project Implicit, "Implicit Association Test," harvard.edu, accessed November 21, 2023, https://implicit.harvard.edu/implicit/Study?tid=-1.

17. Project Implicit, "Implicit Association Test.".

CHAPTER 4

1. Kelly, *The Psychology of Personal Constructs* (London; New York: W. W. Norton & Company, 1955; London; New York: Routledge in association with the Centre for Personal Construct Psychology, 1991).

2. M. Hammer, "The Intercultural Development Inventory: A New Frontier in Assessment and Development of Intercultural Competence," in M. Vande Berg, R. M. Paige, and K. H. Lou, eds., *Student Learning Abroad* (Sterling, VA: Stylus Publishing, 2012), 115–36.

3. Milton J. Bennett, "Towards Ethnorelativism: A Developmental Model of Intercultural Sensitivity," in R. M. Paige, ed., *Education for the Intercultural Experience*, 2nd ed. (Yarmouth, ME: Intercultural Press, 1993).

4. T. Cross, B. Bazron, K. Dennis, and M. Isaacs, *Towards a Culturally Competent System of Care, Volume I* (Washington, DC: Georgetown University Child Development Center, CASSP Technical Assistance Center, 1989).

5. M. Hammer, "The Intercultural Development Inventory."

6. Hammer, "The Intercultural Development Inventory."

7. Wiley, *Validation Analysis of the Intercultural Development Inventory (IDI)* (Las Vegas, NV: ACS Ventures, 2017), https://idiinventory.zendesk.com/hc/en-us/article_attachments/19836951718163.

CHAPTER 5

1. Wiley, *Validation Analysis of the Intercultural Development Inventory (IDI)*. (Las Vegas, NV: ACS Ventures, 2017), https://idiinventory.zendesk.com /hc/en-us/article_attachments/19836951718163.

2. Wiley, *Validation Analysis of the Intercultural Development Inventory (IDI)*.

3. Milton Bennett, "IDI Qualifying Seminar," circa 2001, Minneapolis, MN.

4. Emma Renström, Hanna Bäck, and Royce Carroll, "Threats, Emotions, and Affective Polarization," *Political Psychology* 44, no. 6 (November 2023): 1337–66, https://doi.org/10.1111/pops.12899.

5. "Gun Background Checks Reached New Record during Coronavirus Surge," The Trace, April 1, 2020, https://www.thetrace.org/2020/04 /coronavirus-gun-background-check-record-nics/.

6. Stephen Montemayor, "COVID-19's Spread Fuels Record Run on Guns in Minnesota," *Star Tribune*, accessed November 21, 2023, https://www .startribune.com/covid-19-s-spread-fuels-record-run-on-guns-in-minne sota/569512332/?ref=nl&om_rid=2073762249&om_mid=722272713.

7. Montemayor, "COVID-19's Spread Fuels Record Run on Guns in Minnesota."

8. Simone Weichselbaum and Weihua Li, "As Coronavirus Surges, Crime Declines in Some Cities," *The Marshall Project*, March 27, 2020, https:// www.themarshallproject.org/2020/03/27/as-coronavirus-surges-crime -declines-in-some-cities.

9. City of New York (website), "NYPD Announces Citywide Crime Statistics for March 2020," April 2, 2020, https://www1.nyc.gov/site/nypd /news/p0402b/nypd-citywide-crime-statistics-march-2020.

CHAPTER 6

1. Milton J. Bennett, "Towards Ethnorelativism: A Developmental Model of Intercultural Sensitivity," in R. M. Paige, ed., *Education for the Intercultural Experience*, 2nd ed. (Yarmouth, ME: Intercultural Press, 1993).

CHAPTER 7

1. Mitchell R. Hammer, "Additional Cross-Cultural Validity Testing of the Intercultural Development Inventory," *International Journal of Intercultural Relations* 35, no. 4 (July 2011): 474–87, https://doi.org/10.1016/j.ijintrel.2011.02.014.

2. George Kelly, *The Psychology of Personal Constructs* (London; New York: W. W. Norton & Company, 1955; London; New York: Routledge in association with the Centre for Personal Construct Psychology, 1991).

3. Daniel Cox, Juhem Navarro-Rivera, and Robert P. Jones, "Race, Religion, and Political Affiliation of Americans' Core Social Networks," PRRI, August 3, 2016, https://www.prri.org/research/poll-race-religion-politics-americans-social-networks/.

CHAPTER 8

1. C. Pierce, "Offensive Mechanisms," in F. B. Barbour, ed., *The Black Seventies* (Boston: Porter Sargent, 1970), 265–82.

2. Derald Wing Sue and Lisa Spanierman, *Microaggressions in Everyday Life*, 2nd ed. (Hoboken, NJ: Wiley, 2020).

3. Daniel G. Solórzano and Lindsay Pérez Huber, *Racial Microaggressions in Education: Using Critical Race Theory to Respond to Everyday Racism* (New York: Teachers College Press, 2020).

4. Susan Cousins and Barry Diamond, *Making Sense of Microaggressions* (Open Voices, 2021).

5. Odinakachukwu Ehie, Iyabo Muse, LaMisha Hill, and Alexandra Bastien, "Professionalism: Microaggression in the Healthcare Setting," *Current Opinion in Anaesthesiology* 34, no. 2 (April 2021): 131–36, https://doi.org/10.1097/aco.0000000000000966.

6. Janice McCabe, "Racial and Gender Microaggressions on a Predominantly-White Campus: Experiences of Black, Latina/o and White Undergraduates," *Race, Gender & Class* 16, no. 1/2 (2009): 133–51, https://www.jstor.org/stable/41658864.

7. US Department of Justice, "Law as Microaggression | Office of Justice Programs," www.ojp.gov, https://www.ojp.gov/ncjrs/virtual-library/abstracts/law-microaggression.

8. Tiffany Jana and Michael Baran, *Subtle Acts of Exclusion: How to Understand, Identify, and Stop Microaggressions* (Oakland, CA: Berrett-Koehler Publishers, 2020).

9. Laurie Kelly McCorry, "Physiology of the Autonomic Nervous System," *American Journal of Pharmaceutical Education* 71, no. 4 (August 2007): 78, https://doi.org/10.5688/aj710478.

10. Elyssa Barbash, "Different Types of Trauma: Small 'T' versus Large 'T,'" *Psychology Today*, March 13, 2017, https://www.psychologytoday.com /us/blog/trauma-and-hope/201703/different-types-trauma-small-t -versus-large-t.

11. Barbash, "Different Types of Trauma."

12. Project Implicit, "Preliminary Information," harvard.edu, 2011, https:// implicit.harvard.edu/implicit/takeatest.html. Accessed November 21, 2023.

13. Claude M. Steele and Joshua Aronson, "Stereotype Threat and the Intellectual Test Performance of African Americans," *Journal of Personality and Social Psychology* 69, no. 5 (1995): 797–811, https://doi.org/10 .1037//0022-3514.69.5.797.

CHAPTER 9

1. Jana and Baran, *Subtle Acts of Exclusion: How to Understand, Identify, and Stop Microaggressions* (Oakland, CA: Berrett-Koehler Publishers, 2020).

2. M. R. Hammer, "Solving Problems and Resolving Conflict Using the Intercultural Conflict Style Model and Inventory." In M.A. Moodian, ed., *Contemporary Leadership and Intercultural Competence* (Thousand Oaks, CA: Sage, 2009), 219–32. https://icsinventory.com/resources /mr-hammer-2009-ics-moodian-article .

3. Hammer, "Solving Problems and Resolving Conflict Using the Intercultural Conflict Style Model and Inventory."

4. National Center for Education Statistics, "Race and Ethnicity of Public School Teachers and Their Students," US Department of Education, September 2020, https://nces.ed.gov/pubs2020/2020103/index.asp#:~:text =In%20the%202017%E2%80%9318%20school.

5. National Center for Education Statistics, "Indicator 15: Retention, Suspension, and Expulsion," US Department of Education, updated

February 2019, https://nces.ed.gov/programs/raceindicators/indicator_rda.asp.

6. Emma Hinchliffe, "Women CEOs Run 10.4% of Fortune 500 Companies. A Quarter of the 52 Leaders Became CEO in the Last Year," *Fortune*, June 5, 2023, https://fortune.com/2023/06/05/fortune-500-companies-2023-women-10-percent/.

CHAPTER 10

1. Sara Taylor, *Filter Shift: How Effective People SEE the World* (New York: Morgan James Publishing, 2016).

ACKNOWLEDGMENTS

My gratitude goes first to the deepSEE team, past and present. You have tirelessly supported me in this work to change the world through the workplace. Nick, Sloan, and Namita, thank you for digging for research and sources. Aaron, thank you for your feedback on the manuscript. Your suggestions for core changes have strengthened this book. Meena and Cody, thank you for holding the world back and keeping the business running so I could focus on writing. I couldn't have done it without you!

Without my clients, this book would not be possible. To the hundreds of organizations and countless individuals who have gone through our developmental process, thank you for your questions that forced me to learn new ways of explaining this work. You allowed me to witness your development and learn through your process. Thank you most of all for the trust you placed in me as your guide.

To all of the team at Berrett-Koehler, particularly Steve Piersanti. This book truly would not be what it is without you. Thank you for believing in me and helping me to see beyond a second edition of *Filter Shift*. I am immensely grateful for your tireless commitment to clarity and your supportive guidance.

Thank you to my family. To my kids, thank you for your continual support and love and for your patience with me through this process.

Thank you, Miguel. You are my strongest defender and biggest cheer-leader. I am extremely grateful for your immense love and tireless support.

Finally, I give gratitude to the Divine. Thank you for your guidance, light, and love. I offer this work to you.

INDEX

ABOUT THE AUTHOR

 A little White girl growing up on a farm outside a tiny midwestern town is not someone you would expect to become a diversity, equity, and inclusion (DEI) practitioner. Yet as early as middle school, Sara was researching and giving speeches about differences, prejudices, and stereotypes. Through a steady stream of exchange students in her home, she witnessed significant differences from across the globe.

After college Sara worked in the Dominican Republic, where she began observing her thoughts, judgments, and perspectives as she was living amidst significant differences. The last of her four years there, Sara met Miguel, the engineer assigned by the Dominican government to lead the construction of the canal Sara had been involved with. They married and have raised a beautiful, giving, bicultural, biracial family of four children and one new grandchild—the source of all their pride.

Upon returning to the United States, Sara began work with the University of Minnesota Extension as a diversity and leadership educator and later a diversity specialist. There she took research-based information from the university and made it more applicable and practical to broader audiences outside the academic walls—an approach she has continued throughout her career. Her next role was as a chief diversity officer with Ramsey County in Saint Paul, Minnesota, in the county's first diversity and inclusion office, which gave her the opportunity to build the organization's diversity and inclusion work from the ground up.

In 2002, Sara founded the company she still leads today, deep-SEE Consulting, whose mission is to change the world through the workplace. Through deepSEE, Sara has worked with hundreds of organizations globally to conduct DEI needs assessments, create organizational DEI strategies, conduct countless trainings, and support internal DEI practitioners.

In 1996, Sara obtained her master's degree in Diversity and Organizational Development from the University of Minnesota, where she created her own program through the studies of psychology, cultural competence, organizational development, and systems theory to explore how individuals take in differences as well as how groups and organizations function and can transform.

Sara is a renowned speaker, presenting at national and international conferences as well as with regular client engagements. She has served on the board of the American Heart Association in southwest Minnesota, was a member of the Nobles County Human Rights Commission, and was chair of the board of the nonprofit Multicultural Development Center. Sara has also received numerous awards, including the 2018 People of Distinction Humanitarian Award, and the *Profiles in Diversity Journal's* Women Worth Watching.

Sara and Miguel split their time between their home in the Dominican Republic and their home in Minneapolis, closer to their children and grandchild.

Dear reader,

Thank you for picking up this book and welcome to the worldwide BK community! You're joining a special group of people who have come together to create positive change in their lives, organizations, and communities.

What's BK all about?

Our mission is to connect people and ideas to create a world that works for all.

Why? Our communities, organizations, and lives get bogged down by old paradigms of self-interest, exclusion, hierarchy, and privilege. But we believe that can change. That's why we seek the leading experts on these challenges—and share their actionable ideas with you.

A welcome gift

To help you get started, we'd like to offer you a **free copy** of one of our bestselling ebooks:

www.bkconnection.com/welcome

When you claim your **free ebook**, you'll also be subscribed to our blog.

Our freshest insights

Access the best new tools and ideas for leaders at all levels on our blog at ideas.bkconnection.com.

Sincerely,

Your friends at Berrett-Koehler

MIX
Paper | Supporting
responsible forestry
FSC® C016245

Certified

Corporation